STUDIES IN ENGLISH RHYMES
FROM SURREY TO POPE

STUDIES IN
ENGLISH RHYMES FROM
SURREY TO POPE

A CHAPTER IN THE HISTORY OF ENGLISH

BY

HENRY CECIL WYLD

NEW YORK
RUSSELL & RUSSELL · INC
1965

FIRST PUBLISHED IN 1923
REISSUED, 1965, BY RUSSELL & RUSSELL, INC.
BY ARRANGEMENT WITH JOHN MURRAY, LTD., LONDON
L.C. CATALOG CARD NO: 65—17927
PRINTED IN THE UNITED STATES OF AMERICA

PREFACE

THIS little book is intended primarily for those interested in the study of English literature, of which the problems connected with the rhymes of the earlier poets form a not uninteresting, if subsidiary, study. Most of what is said here will be perfectly familiar to philological students, though, as I have recently discovered, literary students do not always possess the equipment of knowledge and method necessary to deal satisfactorily with some of the questions here discussed. Since the question whether a rhyme, say in Surrey or Shakespeare, was a good one at the time the poem containing it was written can only be settled by an appeal to the facts of pronunciation in the sixteenth century, and often only with reference to still earlier periods of English, it is necessary to bear the history of our language continually in mind if we would deal at all intelligently and fruitfully with the subject. It was therefore impossible to banish from the pages of this book the facts and methods of English philology—these are indeed vital to the whole inquiry. I have tried, however, to make the necessary explanations as clear as possible, to get rid of technical terms, and to assume no knowledge of the history of English on the part of the reader.

I have also made the great concession to literary readers of not using a phonetic notation, though many well-informed persons will consider this omission a piece of folly in a book which is concerned almost entirely with questions of pronunciation. It is certain that by adopting the normal practice in such matters I should have saved myself much trouble, and probably have brought home what I had to say more clearly and precisely to those who were willing to take the trouble to master a simple notation.

However, there is no blinking the fact that, in spite of all the universities now existing in this country, linguistic knowledge and training among the majority of highly cultivated persons are at a very low ebb, and a phonetic notation is a bugbear and an abomination which few, outside the ranks of professed philologists, will face. Therefore, since, as the latter know everything contained in this book, they do not need it, and so probably will not read it, while the others may now venture upon it, which would not have done so had it been disfigured by phonetic symbols. References to the passages whence the rhymes quoted are drawn are not as a rule given. Readers sufficiently interested to turn over the leaves of Spenser, Sackville, and the rest will light on plenty of examples for themselves; and it seemed a pity to disfigure the pages and increase the bulk of so small a book with numerical references to page or line, which few, if any, readers would look out.

I have drawn freely for illustrative material from my own book on *Modern Colloquial English*— I hope I was entitled to do so. The statements of the Grammarians I have derived chiefly from my

own notes on the originals or reprints of their
works, but I have also drawn from Ellis many useful
remarks by Hodges and Price. My admiration
for that great but chaotic book *Early English Pronunciation* was rekindled when I returned to it
again. We should never forget what we owe to Ellis.
He started all of us, directly or indirectly, on the
right path. His arrangement is exasperating; he was
very weak on the historical side of linguistic study;
his *Palæotype*, as he calls his notation, is probably
the worst and most cumbrous ever devised; we differ
nowadays from a very large number of his conclusions—all this is true, but Ellis first showed that
it was possible to know something about the pronunciation of the past, and his own contribution was
colossal. Ellis has examined, in the light of his own
material and his interpretation of it, the rhymes of
Spenser, Shakespeare, Dryden, and other poets.
I found on looking at his remarks again, that things,
as was natural, have moved so much in fifty years
that it was better to work quite independently of
the great man—to collect my own material and
interpret it, to the best of my ability, in my own way.

The same is true of a very interesting study, published as long ago as 1889, *The Versification of Pope*,
by Dr. W. E. Mead, now Professor of English in the
Wesleyan University.

In this book, insufficiently known in this country,
the writer surveys with considerable minuteness
the rhymes of Pope and his immediate predecessors,
and most carefully tests them by the statements of
the Grammarians. Published the year after Sweet's
History of English Sounds, the work represents the

best knowledge and opinions of its day. It is a
great advance, owing to Dr. Mead's philological
training on Ellis's handling of the rhymes of Dryden
and Pope. Many of the writer's conclusions must
have been new in 1889.

I believe the method adopted in the following
pages is sound, and I hope that the unphilological
student will find here some things which he did not
know, and recognise that it is possible to investigate
questions of the kind which are tackled in this book
in a systematic manner, and, by applying a regular
method, to arrive at conclusions which are fairly
certain, at any rate nearer certainty than mere intelli-
gent, bright-eyed, untrained speculation will lead.

For my own part, the most interesting result
which this inquiry has led to is the conviction that
the language of the great poets—and others—of the
sixteenth and seventeenth centuries is a true
mirror, often even in minute details, of the living
spoken English of their age. Hidden beneath a
spelling which too often is as false to reality as our
own, the discerning ear may discover modes of
speech which have long died away, or which have
survived only among clowns. A study of rhymes
may thus reveal to us much that we should never
discover from the perusal of literary prose. This
investigation was pursued, not with a view to discovering the contemporary pronunciation by assuming that most of the rhymes were perfect. It was
rather begun at the other end. The rhymes were
tested, as will be seen, by collateral sources of
information bearing on the pronunciation of the
period. On the whole, then, the poets come out

very well, and not infrequently what seemed at
first sight to be a bad rhyme turned out to be
justified by contemporary statements or spellings;
further, the pronunciation thus suggested, which
made the rhyme a good one, was easily accounted
for by the ' laws ' of English philology.

I have heard the view expressed that we must
not expect the old poets to be too perfect in their
rhymes, that they may often not have aimed at
complete rhymes, but merely at assonance. No
one will question the general possibility of this,
nor that assonances may occur in any period in
English poetry. On the other hand, when, as is
shown repeatedly in the following pages, two
words occurring at the ends of lines are proved
by the testimony of contemporary spellings, as
well as by Grammarians' statements, to have been
pronounced alike by a number of speakers, at
or about the period when the lines were written,
it seems more probable that the poet intended
a real rhyme, as certainly many of his readers
would believe, than that he was thinking of another
pronunciation, also possible in his day, the adoption of which would make a mere assonance. At
the same time it would be very unwise to assume
that Spenser, Shakespeare, Milton, Dryden, and Pope
never made bad rhymes. They certainly did so
now and then, but, I believe, not very often considering the thousands of lines they composed.

HENRY CECIL WYLD.

MERTON COLLEGE, OXFORD.
April, 1923.

WRITERS FROM WHOSE WORKS
THE EXAMPLES OF RHYMES ARE TAKEN.

Rede me and be not wroth. 1529.
Sir Thomas Wyatt. 1503-1542.
Henry, Earl of Surrey. 1517(?)-1547.
Nicholas Udall. (*Roister Doister.*) 1503-1556.
Nicholas Grimald. (Poems in Tottel.) 1519-1562.
Thomas Sackville, Lord Buckhurst. 1536-1608.
Edmund Spenser. (Part of *Faerie Queen* and the other poems.) 1552-1599.
William Shakespeare. (Poems and the Sonnets.) 1564-1616.
Michael Drayton. (Greater part of *Polyolbion*, Sonnets, etc.) 1563-1631.
John Donne. 1573-1631.
William Habington. (*Castara.*) 1605-1654.
Edmund Waller. 1606-1687.
John Milton. 1608-1674.
Sir John Suckling. 1609-1642.
Abraham Cowley. 1618-1667.
John Dryden. 1631-1700.
Jonathan Swift. 1667-1745.
Alexander Pope. 1688-1744.

PRINCIPAL WORKS, CHIEFLY
LETTERS AND DIARIES, QUOTED FOR
ILLUSTRATIVE SPELLINGS.

Letters of **Margaret Paston** (Paston Letters), 1440-1470. Ed. Gairdner.
Chronicle of **William Gregory**, Lord Mayor of London (before) 1467. Camden Society, 1876.
Cely Papers, 1473-1488. Camden Society, 1900.
Henry Machyn's diary, 1550-1553. Camden Society, 1848.
Gabriel Harvey's Letter Book, 1573-1580. Camden Society, 1884.
Queen Elizabeth's letters to James VI., 1582-1602. Camden Society, 1849.

Alleyne Papers, 1580-1661; Memoirs of Edward Alleyne, 1593-1626. Shakespeare Society, 1843.

Mrs. Basire's letters, 1634-1675 (Correspondence of Dr. Basire). Murray, 1831.

Memoirs of the **Verney Family,** 1639-1696. Ed. Lady Verney, 4 vols., 1894.

Wentworth Papers (especially letters of Lady Wentworth, Peter Wentworth, and Lady Strafford), 1705-1739. Ed. Cartwright, 1883.

PRINCIPAL EARLY GRAMMARIANS REFERRED TO.

*(Many of these are quoted at length by Alexander Ellis's
' Early English Pronunciation '; some are reprinted at Halle
by Niemeyer ; others quoted at length by Professor Zachrisson,
' English Vowels from 1400-1700,' Göteborg, 1913.)*

1547. **Salesbury:** Account of English Pronunciation. (Ellis, pp. 768-787.)

1568. **Smith,** Sir Thomas: De Recta et Emendata Linguæ Anglicæ. (Re-ed. Deibel, Halle, 1913.)

1580. **Bullokar:** Booke at large for the amendment of Orthographie for English speech. (Re-ed. Plessow, Palæstra, No. 52, pp. 257, etc.)

1621. **Gill:** Logonomia Anglica. (Re-ed. Jiriczek, Quellen ü Forschungen, No. 90, 1903.)

1634. **Butler:** English Grammar. (Re-ed. Eichler, Halle, 1910.)

1643. **Hodges:** Help to Orthographie. (Cited from Ellis, pp. 1018, etc.)

1653. **Wallis:** Grammatica Linguæ Anglicanæ. (Constantly reprinted during the eighteenth century.)

1668. **Price:** English Orthographie. (Cited from Ellis's extracts, pp. 1024, etc.)

1685. **Cooper:** Grammatica Linguæ Anglicanæ. (Re-ed. Jones, Halle, 1912.)

1701. **Jones:** Practical Phonographer. (Re-ed. Ekwall, Halle, 1907.)

1725. **Baker:** Rules for True Spelling and Writing of English.

CONTENTS

STUDIES IN ENGLISH RHYMES
FROM SURREY TO POPE

CHAPTER I

INTRODUCTION

The Nature and Scope of the Inquiry; Methods and Principles.

IT is remarkable how great is the correspondence between the rhymes used by the poets of the sixteenth and seventeenth centuries with those which, at the present time, everyone would agree in pronouncing perfect. We may read dozens, sometimes perhaps hundreds, of consecutive lines of this verse without discovering more than very few rhymes which appear strange to us. Many imperfect rhymes, such, *e.g.*, as *love–prove*, which occur fairly frequently, are so familiarised by tradition and custom that many readers would hardly recognise them as assonances rather than full, true vowel rhymes. Putting such rhymes as these aside for the moment, it is hardly too much to say that the vast majority of the rhymes of Sackville, Spenser, and Shakespeare are not merely such as would pass muster now, but are of a kind in which the most careful ear could find no flaw. Yet everyone who has thought about the question at all must be aware that English pronunciation has undergone not inconsiderable changes since the sixteenth century. If, therefore, English vowel sounds are somewhat differently pronounced to-day from what they were in the time of Sackville or of Shakespeare, the considerable agreement which exists between the rhymes of their age and that of our own means, and can only mean, that, on the whole, the changes have involved all the words which contain the same sound, and that the vowels in those words which are rhymed by the earlier poets, and which still rhyme perfectly to-day, must have undergone the same changes in pronunciation in all of them. This is no more than the illustration of a cardinal principle of modern philology, which may be briefly formulated as follows: the same sound, in the same dialect, changes at a given time, everywhere in the same way, under the same conditions.

But in spite of the large body of agreement in the matter of rhymes between the old poetry and our own, we cannot read much of the former at all carefully without being struck here and there by considerable discrepancies. When Surrey, for instance, rhymes *bemoan–swolne*; Sackville *depth–leapeth;* Spenser *plot–that, dew–show, beheld–seeld* (seldom); Shakespeare *dally–folly, teeth–with*; when nearly all poets from Sackville to Pope inclusive have rhymes such as *unclean–maintain*, or *dream–name*; when Donne rhymes *burst–dust*, and Waller *height–strait*, are such eccentricities, as we should now regard them, to be set down to carelessness or vulgarity on the part of these poets, to indifference to perfect rhyming, to poetic licence? Were all the above-quoted rhymes really as bad in the sixteenth and seventeenth centuries as they are now, or is there possibly some other explanation ? It is the object of the present inquiry to attempt to give some answer to these questions, and to suggest a sound method of dealing with problems of the kind here raised.

The simple question, in all cases where a rhyme is apparently imperfect, when judged by our present habits of pronunciation, is, Did the poet who produced such a rhyme pronounce both words as we do ? In that case it was a bad rhyme then as now. Or did he pronounce the words so that they really did rhyme ? If he did, and if this was a current mode of pronunciation in his day, then not only was the rhyme a good one so far as the poet himself was concerned, but the great body of his contemporaries also must have felt it to be good. There is always the possibility that a poet might be a provincial or a ' vulgar ' speaker, and that his rhymes might reflect, not the best type of English of his day, but a peculiarity confined to a comparatively small area, or to a limited section of his contemporaries. If this were so, the rhymes of such a poet might still be quite perfect according to his own habits of speech; and if they could be shown to be so, this would throw light on a type of English different in some respects from the standard, but still a real, living form of our language.

Now these questions can only be settled, even approximately, in one way—namely, by an appeal to the past history of English. It is necessary to consider the conditions, not merely of the sixteenth, seventeenth, and eighteenth centuries, but to go behind these, at least to the late fourteenth century,

the age of Chaucer.   There are many things in the
English of the sixteenth century which cannot possibly be understood without some knowledge of
Middle English.   For instance, many of the rhymes
in the sixteenth and seventeenth centuries which are
imperfect from our point of view owe their apparent
discrepancy to the fact that at the present day the
vowel in one of the rhyming words is long, while the
other is short.   Thus Wyatt rhymes *eaten–threaten* ;
Shakespeare, *sweat–heat*; Drayton, *wreath–breath*;
Donne, *great–get*; Milton, *spreads–meads*; and so on.
But in Middle English all these words have a long
vowel, and there is independent evidence that many
of them continued to be pronounced, by numerous
speakers, with a long vowel far into the seventeenth
century (see pp. 88, 89).

There are other words used as rhymes whose
vowels, if the rhymes were good, must have had a
different quantity from that which they have to-day,
where the difference is due to phonetic conditions arising, in Middle English, from the presence of inflexional
endings.   For instance, the Positive *grēte*, ' great,'
has a long vowel in Middle English; that of the
Comparative *grettre* (later *gretter*) is short.   It is a
well-established fact that in Middle English a long
vowel followed by -*tr*-, and by many other consonantal
combinations, is shortened.   We know also from such
spellings as *gretter* that this old form of the Comparative survived in the sixteenth century.   Therefore when Spenser rhymes *get her–greater* we consider it likely, in spite of the spelling, that he is
using the old Comparative with a short vowel,
and that the rhyme is perfect.   It is probable that

the number of people interested in the rhymes of Spenser and Shakespeare is much larger than that of those qualified by training and special knowledge to pronounce any judgment upon the innumerable problems involved in a study of this not unimportant aspect of English literature. For the whole question is one which demands sound and exact special knowledge, and the application of a rigorous philological method.

Without an accurate knowledge of the phonology and grammar of Middle English, and of the fifteenth and sixteenth centuries, without a training in the methods of English philological inquiry, and some experience in the application of such method to the special problems of English pronunciation during the period from Chaucer to Pope, it is unfortunately impossible to form any but the haziest and most incorrect notions on the subject. It is one thing to observe facts, it is quite another to interpret them properly.

Many rhymes which occur in the works of the early poets appear inharmonious and irregular; the poets are often inconsistent in their own practice. There are a certain number of rhymes which defy the most careful scrutiny, and the most liberal allowance for possible variants of pronunciation, to bring them into accord with the usage of the period to which they belong. These are difficulties which a trained student has to face. But if the inquirer is improperly equipped for his task, he is likely to be very constantly pulled up and baffled by what he conceives to be the indifference of the poets to good rhymes. On the other hand, the student who is aware of the standards of pronunciation of the various ages

discovers, often perhaps to his surprise, how faithfully, on the whole, these are reflected in the rhymes.
The study of rhymes, if pursued in the right way,
with the necessary equipment of knowledge, and the
means of testing the apparent incongruities, becomes
a task of the highest interest. It soon becomes
manifest from collateral evidence, that the language
of the poets is a true mirror of the speech of their
age, with all its fashions, its affectations, its queer
survivals from the past, and its stirrings of what
is to be the unquestioned standard of the future.

It will not be attempted here to prove that the old
poets never rhymed amiss; that they were always
perfect craftsmen. Our aim is to discover the truth
so far as may be possible. It is suggested that,
however ' bad ' a rhyme of the age of Shakespeare,
Dryden, and Pope may appear when judged simply
by the standards of our own usage, we are not justified in dismissing it as imperfect and careless until
we have tested it in the most searching way, and
by every means at our disposal. If all these fail
to establish the actual existence, or even the probability, of such a pronunciation in the poet's own
day as would make the rhyme a good one, then,
and not till then, are we entitled to say that
the rhyme is faulty. Now the result of applying
rigid tests to a very large number of rhymes which,
at the first blush, appear imperfect, has been
to show that the vast majority of these doubtful
rhymes were perfectly sound and good. The
residuum of rhymes which, so far as the present
writer could discover, admitted of no satisfactory
explanation was comparatively slight.

The Nature of the Apparent Discrepancies.

The first thing to do is to classify the apparent defects in a more or less systematic manner. The following is believed to cover the larger number, and the more important types of apparent imperfection.

A. **Rhymes affecting the vowels:** (1) Differences in the vowel character or *Quality* in rhymed words; (2) differences of vowel *Quantity*.

B. **Rhymes affecting consonantal sounds :** (1) Loss of consonants; (2) substitution of one consonant for another.

C. **Isolated words:** There are a certain number of these which require special treatment.

Let us now consider what means we have of testing the character of the rhymes—that is to say, what are the sources of information about the pronunciation of the past.

The Tests.

The following kinds of collateral evidence are available:

1. General considerations based on our knowledge of the history of English prior to the period of the poet we are considering.

2. The poetical usage and tradition prior to and contemporary with the poet.

3. The statements of writers on English pronunciation round about the period covered by the poet's life.

4. The testimony of the **Occasional Spellings**

found in unstudied private documents, especially
private letters, diaries, etc., but also in more public
documents, and even, occasionally, in printed books
from the fifteenth to the eighteenth centuries. These
spellings, of which more shortly, are often unconsciously phonetic in character and throw a wonderful
light upon contemporary pronunciation.

5. Survivals in our own or earlier periods of an
older usage, which may occur in popular forms of
speech, though now considered vulgar, provincial,
or old-fashioned in standard English.

We may deal briefly with these points in order.

1. Considerations Based on the Earlier History of English.

A fundamental error into which we are apt to
fall in judging of the rhymes of the sixteenth and
seventeenth centuries is to think of them in terms
of the usage with which we are acquainted in our
own day. We forget, when we do this, that the writers
of two or three hundred years ago, could not possibly
anticipate the standards which would obtain long
after they were dead, nor foresee what was the path
of development which English was going to follow
in days which had not yet dawned. They therefore
were not writing and rhyming in accordance with
the visionary linguistic usage of a remote posterity,
but according to the familiar habits of their own day,
guided, doubtless, also by the tradition derived from
their forerunners in poetic craft. This is obvious
as soon as it is stated, but it is desirable to state it,
and to insist that the fact of a rhyme being bad at

the present time has no necessary bearing on the question whether it was so in the days of Shakespeare or of Milton. In judging the rhymes of Pope, it is not quite so misleading to apply the present standards, because the changes in usage since his day have been far slighter than during the longer period since Shakespeare.

It is essential in estimating the rhymes of the sixteenth and seventeenth centuries to know whence the language came, from what it had developed. The pronunciation and the grammatical forms of the sixteenth century have grown by a series of regular changes from those of Chaucer's day. The former preserve many features of the latter which we have now lost. This is particularly noticeable in respect of quantity (see pp. 86, etc.). A whole series of lengthenings and shortenings of vowels, which have produced forms that appear to us, from our present standpoint, the only possible ones, were altogether unknown in Chaucer's time, so far as we know, and were only slowly making good their position in the standard language in the age of Surrey, of Sackville, and of Shakespeare.

Again, owing to various circumstances—the influence of other dialects, phonetic conditions arising in inflexion, or the incidence of stress in the sentence or in the single word—doublets as they are called, that is two forms of the same word, often came into being. The writers of the sixteenth and seventeenth centuries may use either or both of such forms; but the one they prefer as being the more usual type in their day is by no means always that which is current now. Without a refer-

ence to the facts of Middle English, the existence
of one of these variants would never be suspected,
and we may censure a sixteenth-century poet for
rhyming a word with another of which we now only
know one type, whereas the poet we are criticising
may have been using another type altogether, one
of whose existence we are unaware, but which constituted a perfect rhyme.   Ignorance in these matters
disqualifies a critic from coming to the right conclusion about a very large class of early rhymes.

2. Poetical Tradition.

Two considerations arise in connection with
poetical tradition.   In the first place, when we
find writer after writer in a given age making
use of the same constructions, words, and grammatical forms, it is a fair inference, unless the
contrary be proved by other irrefragable evidence,
that those words, forms, and constructions are part
and parcel of the common usage of the age, that
they belong and conform to current contemporary
practice.   One writer here or there may play
pranks, and try new-fangled experiments, but we
shall hardly find all his contemporaries imitating
him in his eccentricities.   The same line of argument may, up to a point, be applied to the rhymes
of a period.   It is scarcely possible to conceive a
conspiracy among poets to spoil their verse by adopting bad rhymes, and the same bad rhymes.   It
seems reasonable, then, to argue that when a certain
class of rhymes recur in the poetry of an age there
is an a priori presumption that these rhymes were

' good ' and satisfactory to the ears of poets and readers in that age.

This is one side. The other raises a curious and interesting subject of inquiry. No one doubts that the poets of every age are nurtured in the schools of their older contemporaries, and of their immediate and remoter predecessors. Just as the instrument on which the artist plays—that is, the language of each generation—grows out of that which has gone before, so also does the melody, the style, spring from a long line of earlier crafts-men; but it is re-coined in the mint of living speech as spoken by the writer and the men of his time. This is to say that a poet may continue to rhyme words together, after they have ceased to be true rhymes, because such rhymes are traditional, and occur again and again in the verse of his predecessors. The usage has changed; other types prevail in the current speech of living men; but certain rhymes, once perfect, now become false, may still be used because of the sanction afforded by poetical tradition. This adherence to outworn traditional rhymes is greatly encouraged when the words to be coupled in rhyme agree in their spelling, when they constitute what are called *rhymes to the eye*. Many rhymes of this type are in vogue to-day— *love–prove, flood–brood, hear–bear, waste–past, have–grave*, and so on. All these are *eye-rhymes*; they occur in the best poets; they are convenient. What more is necessary ? It may be asserted that all of the above pairs once rhymed perfectly, and it is probably true to say that hardly any of the rhymes of this class, now so familiar that only the most scrupulous are struck by them, would have passed into common poetic usage at all, had they not once been true rhymes to the ear, as well as to the eye. The tradition is rooted in the habits of pronunciation of a former age.

It is a nice question to decide just when, in what generation, a given traditional rhyme ceases to be a true one. How far was Pope merely reproducing Dryden in those cases when his (Pope's) rhymes appear to us faulty, and how far was he really reflecting the pronunciation of his own age ? To such a question no general answer can be given. It is purely a question of collateral evidence bearing on the pronunciation of Pope's day.

On the whole it is safe to say that most poets are conservative and prefer to adhere to tradition, if not too remote, even when the results are unsatisfactory, rather than to be too modern, and reflect the actual pronunciation of their own day so faithfully, that their rhymes, though perfect, do not appeal to the eye, and flout ancient tradition. This is true, at least, of the great poets of the past, though perhaps less so of the mob of gentlemen who write with difficulty at the present time. A significant case of conservatism in rhyming on the part of the old poets is that of the *wand–hand* class (see pp. 67–70 below).

None of the seventeenth-century poets apparently, before Dryden, ever rhyme *wand*, say, with *pond*, and Dryden himself has very few of such rhymes—that is, of words spelt *wa-*, etc., with others spelt with *o*. All the poets continue to rhyme *wand–hand, reward–hard*, etc., long after these had ceased to rhyme in ordinary pronunciation, and they avoid such rhymes as *war–sore*, though this was as perfect then as now. Until quite recently many poets boggled at *morning–dawning*, *Lord–awed*, because of the difference in spelling, but rhymed *Lord–word* without scruple, as indeed many hard-pressed rhymesters still do.

3. Statements of Early Writers on English Pronunciation.

From the end of the first third of the sixteenth century onwards, numerous writers, British and foreign, deal descriptively with the English pronunciation of their own day. These writers, who will henceforth be referred to as the Grammarians, vary greatly in their character, qualifications, and aims. Some wish to describe English pronunciation for foreigners; some are Grammarians who deal with pronunciation as part of English Grammar: these insist strongly upon what they conceive to be ' correct,' and characterise certain pronunciations as ' barbarous,' others as ' affected '; other writers, again, are primarily interested in proposing a new system of spelling, and give passages, printed according to their system. Among the most helpful of the sixteenth-century writers on pronunciation are foreigners who, having no special prejudices, as have most of the English writers of that time, against describing faithfully a pronunciation which departs greatly from the spelling, often reveal the truth which our own countrymen are inclined to conceal.

If we are bent on discovering the precise character of the vowel sounds in the sixteenth century, we

shall generally be disappointed in what the writers
of that day have to tell us.   Their usual method is
to compare the sounds represented by this or that
letter, in English, with the nearest sound in French,
Welsh, Italian, etc.   At best such a method can
only give an approximate notion of the facts, and
we are sometimes inclined to doubt whether the
writer is really perfectly acquainted with the sounds
of both of the languages which he is comparing.
The general tendency of most of the earliest writers
is in the direction of refusing to admit that the
English spelling of the sixteenth century no longer
expressed the pronunciation of the time.   Some of
them represent the ' continental values ' of the
vowels as still surviving in ordinary English, although
from other sources we can be certain that these had
long vanished.

Altogether, these writers are in many ways dis-
appointing, and their testimony as regards the actual
pronunciation of vowels is often misleading.   On
the other hand, they generally give lists of English
words which have the same sound, and this is perhaps
the most useful contribution which most of the
Grammarians and Orthoëpists down to the first half
of the seventeenth century are able to make to our
knowledge.   With Wallis (1654) and Cooper (1685)
we find the opening of a new era in the description
of actual pronunciation, in acuteness of observa-
tion, and in freedom from prejudice.   For our
present purpose it is often enough if a writer states
that such and such words have the same vowel
sound.   Particularly useful are the list of Hodges
(1643) of ' Such words as are alike in sound and unlike

both in their signification and writing,' and that of Price (1668) of the same sort. Cooper is more critical than the other two, and distinguishes between words which are sounded alike, and those whose pronunciation is *nearly* alike. Some of the later we may suspect to have been in reality generally pronounced completely alike in Cooper's day, though he chose to recommend that a difference should be made as being more ' correct.' For instance, he puts *stricter–stricture* in the list of words *nearly* alike, and yet includes *pickt her–picture* among those having the same pronunciation. We know from other sources that the ending *-ture* was commonly pronounced like *-ter* in Cooper's day, and probably for several centuries before it. We may therefore suppose that for some reason Cooper chose to reject a pronunciation in one word which he accepts in another. It is a significant fact that Cooper should associate together certain words as *nearly* alike in sound, as a kind of warning against pronouncing them *exactly* alike. Unless, in some types of pronunciation, the words actually were pronounced alike, the warning and the lists would both be unnecessary. In fact, in some cases, though not in all, it is pretty certain that many people in Cooper's day did pronounce alike the pairs of words between which he indicates a mere resemblance, though not an identity of pronunciation. It is a common experience to find certain pronunciations denounced by the Grammarians as ' barbarous,' or ' incorrect,' which we have other reasons for knowing were current among well-bred speakers.

It sometimes happens that a Grammarian gives us

more information when enumerating types of pronunciation which he censures, than when he is attempting to describe what he asserts is ' correct.'

As regards the bearing of the statements of the Grammarians on the rhymes, the latter sometimes suggest that the poet must have had the type of pronunciation which is condemned by one or more contemporary, or nearly contemporary, writers as ' barbarous' or ' low.' The mere mention, however, of such a type, though it be but with dispraise, is enough to prove that it existed.

Great caution is needed in accepting the statement of one of these writers that such and such a pronunciation is ' vulgar.' We do not always know in what world he formed his standards, nor what company he kept. In some circles, at the present day, it may be considered elegant to pronounce a *t* in *often*, whereas in others, to do so would be regarded as a ridiculous vulgarism.

The evidence afforded by the next source of information we shall discuss, the *Occasional Spellings*, does not by any means confirm, in all cases, the views of the Grammarians as to what is ' barbarous' and ' incorrect.' We have plenty of indications that in a social world considerably above that in which most of them lived, much that the Grammarians condemn was current in the speech of the sixteenth and seventeenth centuries.

For instance, Cooper puts down as words which are pronounced ' nearly alike' *value* and *volley*. Why? No one would assert that at the present time they are pronounced in such a way as to resemble each other much more than *cat* resembles *coat*. What is

Cooper thinking of? Against what is he warning his readers? It can be shown that in the seventeenth century many good speakers pronounced the first vowel in *volley* exactly as they pronouced the first vowel in *valley*. Even Shakespeare must have pronounced the first vowel in *folly* in this way— as '*fally*' (see pp. 71, 72).

Again, nothing is more certain than that the syllable -*ue*, or -*ew*, was pronounced like -*y* when unstressed. The verb *value* is spelt *valy* in a letter of Lady Sussex, in 1642, and in the same way Mrs. Basire writes *neuie* for 'nephew' in 1655. Cooper knew perfectly well that thousands of good speakers in his day pronounced *volley* and *value* alike as 'valley,' but for some reason he did not choose to face the fact. We must not, however, be ungrateful to Cooper; he is freer than any writer of his kind before, and than some who followed him, from the besetting sin of his tribe—namely, a tendency to describe the language, not as it really is, but according to an ideal conception of what it ought to be. He also deserves a handsome tribute for his phonetic knowledge, which was far in advance of that of his contemporaries and of his successors for many generations. The influence exerted by those Grammarians of the sixteenth and seventeenth centuries who endeavoured to correct what they conceived to be the faults of speech of their contemporaries was, so far as can be discovered, of the slightest possible kind. Upon the fashionable speakers, who, after all, were those who unconsciously created, by their usage, the type of spoken English which had the greatest prestige and currency among the gay world of the Court and the upper reaches of society, their influence must have been nil.

Nor would it be in accordance with probability to suppose that the poets studied the crabbed works which professed to set forth how English ought to be pronounced, and made their rhymes on a prescribed model. We cannot, for various reasons, imagine this of Surrey, or Sackville, or Spenser, or Milton, or Dryden. There certainly was no league between poets and Grammarians whereby these led, and those followed in the matter of rhyme. The two worked independently of each other. If this is so, we are entitled, when we find the usage of the poets coinciding with the accounts given by the Grammarians of agreement in sound between certain words, to regard the two sources as independent and as confirming each other. It sometimes happens that the very same words used by the poets in rhyme are mentioned by the Grammarians in a way which points to the pronunciation being that which we should have to assume for the rhyme to be perfect. Thus, for example, when Dryden rhymes *fate–height*, and Baker, writing a quarter of a century later, says that *height* is pronounced *hate*, it seems reasonable to suppose that Dryden may have pronounced the word in this way, and that his rhyme was perfect. It is for the English philologist of the present day to show how this pronunciation came about, and to explain the historical relation of this type to that other which is current to-day. Again, if Swift rhymes *meat–say't*, and Cooper, writing when Swift was eighteen years of age, says that *meat* is pronounced like *mate*, we can hardly be in doubt as to what Swift's pronunciation of the former word was.

The Grammarians, then, in spite of their defects, are often able to throw a very valuable light on our problems, and to provide information which is quite conclusive for our purpose. Finally, it may be mentioned that their usual intense conservatism in speech, and their dislike for novelty and eccentricity, should incline us to put confidence in their statements when these are confirmed from any other source.

4. The Occasional Spellings of a Phonetic Character.

This source of information, in many ways the most important and enlightening of all those upon which we levy toll, so far as concerns the Modern Period, is available from the second quarter of the fifteenth century onwards.

The kind of spellings referred to are those which depart from the traditional and conventional spelling of the time, and which rise unconsciously to the pen of the writer who is, so to speak, uttering mentally the words which he is putting on paper. These spellings occur in large numbers first in the fifteenth century, chiefly because at that time there was a large increase in the number of ordinary persons of all classes who wrote their letters with their own hands, instead of invoking the services of a professional scribe. Among some of the most valuable collections of letters and other documents of this kind we may mention the Paston Letters; the Cely Papers—letters of a family of Essex wool

merchants (1473-1488); Shillingford Papers (1447-
1450)—the letters of John Shillingford, Mayor of
Exeter; the Chronicle of William Gregory, Lord
Mayor of London, written before 1467; numerous
letters of the fifteenth and sixteenth centuries in Sir
Henry Ellis's *Original Letters Illustrative of English
History* (3 series, 3 vols. in each); Lord Berners's
translation of Froissart, 1520; Sir Thomas Elyot's
Booke of the Gouernour, 1531; Diary of Henry
Machyn, 1550-1553; Gabriel Harvey's Letter Book,
1573-1580; Lady Hungerford's Letters, 1560-1588,
in *Society in the Elizabethan Age*, Hubert Hall;
Queen Elizabeth's Letters to James VI., also her
Translations; the Alleyne Papers, 1580-1661—
Memoirs of Edward Alleyne, 1593-1626; Memoirs of
the Verney Family (4 vols.), 1639-1696; Letters of
Lady Wentworth, in Wentworth Papers, 1705-1739.

In addition to these, which include some works
of literature, there is much valuable material in the
State Papers of Henry VIII., and, speaking generally,
almost every book published in the sixteenth century
contains a certain number of spellings which are
important as throwing light on the pronunciation
of the day.

It must not be supposed that it is only more or
less uneducated persons, or those whose interests
lie rather in practical affairs than in literature, who
lapse from the orthodox mode of spelling. In the
sixteenth century the letters of Sir Thomas More, the
sermons of Latimer, the letters and literary work of
Sir Thomas Smith, the works of Ascham and of Lily,
the letters of Gabriel Harvey, and those of Queen
Elizabeth, all abound with more or less phonetic

spellings.   Apart from the letters of the Celys, the
chronicle of Gregory, and the diary of Machyn,
nearly all the documents referred to which are not
literary works published during, or shortly after the
author's lifetime, are the production of persons of
the upper class, and we have therefore a fairly long
first-hand record of the speech of that class.

It is desirable to illustrate here the kind of information we can gather from these unstudied private
documents, in which the writers, while generally
adhering to such rules of spelling as they have learnt,
frequently unconsciously deviate from them.

Vowel Sounds.—The spellings show that already in
the fifteenth century the old ' continental ' quality of
the English vowels had passed away and that in many
cases something on the way to, or identical with, the
present-day sounds had already been reached.

M.E. *ā*, often written *e*: *credyll*, ' cradle '
(Bokenam's Poems, *c.* 1443); *ceme*, ' came ' (Cely
Papers); *teke*, ' take ' (Paston Letters).

M.E. *ā* and M.E. *ai*, written interchangeably:
maid, ' made ' (Coventry Leet Book, 1421); *saive*,
' save ' (State Papers of Henry VIII., 1515); *waiter*,
' water ' (Leics. Will, 1539); *maik*, ' make' (Queen
Elizabeth); *panes*, ' pains ' (Anne Boleyn, 1528);
agane (Queen Elizabeth); *pade*, ' paid ' (Lady Sussex
in Verney Memoirs, 1642).

M.E. *ē*[1] written *y*, *i*, to express present sound:
myte, ' meet ' (Shillingford); *symed*, ' seemed '
(Margaret Paston); *stypylle*, ' steeple ' (Gregory's
Chronicle, etc.).

M.E. *ē*[2] written *a*, showing retention of old
continental ' sound: *retrate*, ' retreat ' (Spenser,

'Faerie Queen'); *discrate*, 'discreet' (Verney
Memoirs, 1655).

M.E. *ī* and *oi* written alike—*i* or *y* for *oi*, *oi* for *ī*:
pyson, 'poison' (Gregory); *gine*, 'join' (Verney
Memoirs, 1656); *regis*, 'rejoice' (Mrs. Basire, 1654,
etc.); *defoyled*, 'defiled' (Monk of Evesham, 1482,
etc.).

M.E. *-er-* written *-ar-*. There are a large number
of these spellings from the fifteenth to eighteenth
centuries (see *Hist. Coll. Engl.*, p. 217 ff.). A few
examples will suffice here: *sarten*, etc., 'certain'
(Cely Papers, Gregory, Verney Memoirs, Mrs.
Basire, Lady Wentworth); *darth*, 'dearth' (Lord
Berners, Thomas Wilson, 1560); *divart*, *divarsion*
(Verney Memoirs, 1686); *larne*, 'learn' (Verney
Memoirs, 1647, 1652); *marcy*, 'mercy' (Gregory,
Gabriel Harvey, Queen Elizabeth, Lady Sussex,
Verney Memoirs, 1642, Mrs. Basire, 1654, etc.);
parson, 'person' (Margaret Paston, Lord Berners,
Sir Thomas Elyot's Will, Machyn, Queen Elizabeth,
Lady Sussex, 1641, Dr. Denton, Verney Memoirs,
1660, Lady Wentworth, etc.).

Vowels in Unstressed Syllables.—These are less
important for our present purpose, but it may be
mentioned here that it is evident from a long
series of occasional spellings, beginning in the
fifteenth century, that from that time onwards
something very like our present system of 'slurring'
unaccented vowels was current. In some cases—
e.g., those mentioned above (p. 17)—we have
now 'restored' a supposed 'correct' pronunciation
through the influence of the official spelling. We have
retained the old pronunciation of French *u* in *biscuit*

(-*it*), and *minute* (of time, or a note), which is spelt *minite* in the fifteenth century, but have ' restored ' a (new) sound in the unstressed syllable of *fortune*, for which (mysse)*forten* occurs in Machyn (1550), and *fortin*, etc., half a dozen times in the Verney Memoirs.

Peculiarities of the Consonantal Sounds. — *Substitution*: -*in* for -*ing* (very frequent from sixteenth to eighteenth centuries; noted in fourteenth).

-*ft* for -*ght*: *dafter* (Verney Memoirs, 1629, 1645, 1657); *boft* (Jones, a writer on pronunciation, 1701).

-*f* and *v* written for -*th*: *erf*, ' earth ' (Book of Quintessence, *c.* 1460-1470); *Lambeffe* (Gregory), *bequived*, ' bequeathed ' (Queen Elizabeth).

Assimilation: -*ti*-, -*si*-, -*su*-, written -*sh*-, -*ch*-: *fessychens*, ' physicians ' (Cely Papers); *instrocshens*, ' instructions ' (Sir Thomas Seymour, 1544); *ishu*, ' issue ' (Gabriel Harvey); *suspishiously* (Lady Verney, Verney Memoirs, 1646); *sheute*, ' suit ' (Alleyne Papers, 1593, etc.).

Loss of Consonant: Loss of *r*, especially before -*s*: *mosselle* (Gregory); *skasely*, ' scarcely ' (Sir Thomas Seymour, 1544); *Dasset*, ' Dorset ' (Machyn, 1550); *posshene*, ' portion ' (1593); *passons*, ' persons ' (Mrs. Isham, Verney Memoirs, 1642); *Gath*, ' Garth ' (Lady Wentworth).

Loss of -*t*: *offen*, ' often ' (Queen Elizabeth); *wascote* (Edward Alleyne, 1593); *busling*, ' bustling ' (Sir P. Warwick, 1701); *excep* (Cely Papers); *prompe* (Ascham, *Toxophilus*); *Egype* (Machyn); *stricklier* (Alleyne Papers, 1608); *respeck* (Mrs. Isham, 1642, etc.).

Addition of Consonant: *d* or *t* added after final

n, l, s, f: *lynand,* ' linen ' (Capgrave, fifteenth century); *loste,* ' loss ' (Gregory); *synst* (R. Pace to Wolsey, *c.* 1515); *varment,* ' vermin ' (Thomas Pery, 1539); *surgiant,* ' surgeon ' (Gabriel Harvey); *micklemust,* ' Michaelmas ' (Verney Memoirs, 1642, etc.).

Such are a few samples of the kind of spellings which are scattered up and down the private letters and diaries of the period between the middle of the fifteenth century and the middle of the eighteenth. Some of the pronunciations are only expressed in this phonetic manner a few times, and the instances are separated by long intervals; others recur, with an almost identical spelling, again and again through the centuries. It is very significant that we find the same spelling cropping up several times in the letters of persons who lived at quite different periods, and to note how these spellings suggest a pronunciation which we have ourselves heard, or even, perhaps, use. Many spellings diverge so widely from the traditional that they cannot be mere attempts to reproduce the ' correct ' forms which the writer has partly forgotten. They are obviously quite independent of the regular spellings and have an entirely different basis. They are, in fact, as has been said, due to the writer unconsciously putting down the nearest representation of his own pronunciation which came to his pen. A striking confirmation of the value of these occasional spellings, as revelations of the actual speech of the time, is that the Grammarians, in attempting to make clear the nature of a pronunciation to which they wish to draw attention, sometimes make use of the same spelling as we find in our careless letter-writers. The study of the occasional spellings has of recent years considerably altered our views on the approximate period during which our present vowel sounds developed. Formerly, students of the Modern Period of English relied almost entirely upon the testimony of the Grammarians, with the result that the present vowel sounds were supposed to have emerged anything from a hundred to two hundred years later than we are now inclined to place their development. Concerning the vowels in unstressed syllables, the Grammarians give us no information before the seventeenth century, and then only of a very unsatisfactory kind. As for the many strange developments in the pronunciation of combinations of consonants, something may be gathered from the Grammarians from Cooper onwards, but several phenomena which are hinted at by the writers of the late seventeenth and early and later eighteenth centuries are shown by the spellings of the kind we are considering to have been in existence centuries earlier. It is, in fact, impossible to construct anything like a complete picture of the external, audible side of English speech during the sixteenth and seventeenth centuries, from the pages of the Grammarians alone. When we become immersed in the intimate private letters of these centuries, so that we begin to grasp the meaning of the phonetic spellings, we feel almost as though we could hear the distant voices of the past ringing in our ears. The priceless collection of letters in the Verney Memoirs is worth all the Grammarians of the seventeenth rhyme *health–self*, and on p. 114 with reference to Surrey's rhyme *swolne–bemoan*.

When we consider the excellent lead which many generations of men and women of the world gave in the direction of a real reform of English spelling— a reform which would have made it practically phonetic instead of being, as it now is, perhaps the worst in Europe, as a representation of the pronunciation—it may seem surprising that our spelling should have survived these assaults of common sense, and have become crystallised, to all intents and purposes, with the main features which it bore in the fourteenth century, when it was already rapidly becoming obsolete. It is evident that the natural tendency in the fifteenth and sixteenth centuries, and later, among all classes, high and low, learned and unlearned, was to bring the spelling more in harmony with the functions which it was supposed to fulfil. Very little encouragement on the part of the printers of books would have been enough. The unsophisticated natural ' mistakes ' which we find repeated from age to age were, on the whole, both simpler and more expressive than the elaborate attempts at reformed spelling which were made from time to time, often by pedants, and which found no response among the public at large. It is doubtful, indeed, whether more than a handful of readers perused the works of Smith, Bullokar, and Gill. The responsibility for fixing our spelling just at the wrong time, must rest with early printers. Caxton, with all his incontestable merits, was a man of somewhat limited vision and imagination. He simply took over the spelling of the professional scribes and made no changes of any significance. It is too late now. The vast army of readers has long formed its habits and does not want to alter them. The majority of educated people regard our spelling as something sacred, and almost believe that to tamper with it would be to strike a deadly blow at the language which it is supposed to preserve. It is easy to bring forward arguments in favour of reform, many of which are unassailable on purely rational grounds. But these are as nothing against the huge body of sentiment, custom, and prejudice which will probably always prevail against any proposed change in a system which everybody has grown accustomed to. Most of those whose main occupation is the study of philological problems, of which the relation of speech to spelling is one, and who are perhaps free from prejudice in the matter, would probably be unwilling to embark upon a crusade for orthographical reform, partly because they are themselves indifferent, partly on account of the opposition which it would encounter, and the flood of tedious argument for and against which would inevitably be loosed if there were any serious danger of the movement succeeding.

As it is, English spelling has exercised considerable influence upon English pronunciation during the last century or so, and it is impossible to foresee how much further this will go. It is germain to our present purpose to mention this, because one of the strangest results has been the love for 'eye-rhymes,' the beginnings of which we shall have occasion to note in the sixteenth century (pp. 56, 57). Although the poets of that age preferred that rhymes which were perfect to the ear should also appeal to the eye, it is not to be supposed that the readers thought much about it, seeing the fluid state in which even the spelling of the printers then was.

It is very doubtful whether good poets in the sixteenth century ever rhymed words together, simply on account of similar spelling, and irrespective of the sound. In the later seventeenth century this may have happened, but as a general practice, this kind of ' poetic licence ' could only be the product of a generation who read more than they spoke, and for whom language was something rather to be *looked at* than *listened to*. Such persons are fortunately rare in any age.

We have now considered the chief tests whereby the rhymes of the old poets may be judged. The remaining one of those enumerated above is not nearly so important as the others, and in itself would not be conclusive. Taken in conjunction with the testimony of the Grammarians, and that afforded by the Occasional Spellings, it may, however, have some confirmatory value, and may therefore be briefly alluded to.

5. Survivals of Earlier Types of Pronunciation in Existing Popular Dialects.

Everyone is familiar with the Irish pronunciation in which *heat, meat, eat* are identical in sound with *hate, mate, ate* respectively, and there are dozens of words in which the same difference is heard between the Irish brogue and Standard English. This is undoubtedly a survival, in Irish pronunciation, of the common English pronunciation of the seventeenth and eighteenth centuries. (On this question see p. 51, etc.) It can be quite conclusively established that this feature of Irish-English is not a new departure.

In most of the popular dialects the ending -*ing* is still pronounced -*in*. This habit, so common among poets far into the nineteenth century, is not a modern alteration of the Standard Language, but a survival of a feature which formerly was almost universal, and which still survives among many well-bred and highly educated speakers (p. 112).

The identification of 'long *i*' and *oi* which we find in the poets, in the Occasional Spellings, and in the writings of the Grammarians (see pp. 73–75) is still common among many speakers of regional dialects, who pronounce *oil* and *isle* exactly alike.

The 'un-rounding' of 'short *o*'—that is, the pronunciation of this sound as 'short *a*'—established by every one of our sources from the sixteenth to eighteenth centuries (pp. 70–72), is still a well-marked feature of the South-Western and South-Western Midland dialects of England. The variety in the distribution of the sounds now heard in Standard English, respectively in *glove* on the one hand, and *moon* on the other, which, apparent in the rhymes of the early poets (pp. 75–82), still exists in the popular dialects, whose usage in this respect by no means always conforms to that of the Standard.

The Application of the Tests.

It will be agreed, probably, that where it is possible to apply all the above tests to a particular rhyme in an early poet, and where the evidence of all

points in the same direction—namely, to the existence of a pronunciation which would make the rhyme
a good one—we may, without further hesitation,
accept the result as conclusive, and assume that
the rhyme in question was perfect.

Failing such complete evidence, which is not always
available, we may in general be content with less.
If a rhyme is supported by the Occasional Spellings,
or by the Grammarians alone, this should usually
be enough, especially when the pronunciation thus
made probable is capable of explanation by the
ordinary principles of English philology. The
' faulty ' spellers of the sixteenth and seventeenth
centuries could have no intention of misleading a
posterity whom they had no notion would ever read
what they wrote; the Grammarians were not in league
with the poets to support bad rhymes by statements
which were at variance with plain facts. Nor did
the poets base their rhymes upon the rules of the
Grammarians.

Poets, Grammarians, and writers of private letters
and diaries worked independently of each other,
and when any two of them tell the same tale we
cannot reasonably withhold credence.

Existence of Variant Pronunciations during the Same Period.

It will probably strike the reader who is unaccus-
tomed to the minute study of the earlier periods of
our language, that in the discussions of the various
problems arising from our inquiry, more than one
pronunciation of a word is assumed to have existed
at the same time, and that both are sometimes used

by the same poet on different occasions.   This may
appear to many a surprising assumption.   Surely,
they will say, a great poet would know the ' correct '
usage of his time, would adopt it, if it were not naturally his own, and would stick to it.   If a standard
of correctness or of ' bel usage ' was recognised at
all, it would involve one thing or the other; if this
one was ' right,' that other must have been regarded
as vulgar or provincial.

What sort of a standard could that be which per-
mitted variant pronunciations of the same word ?
What sort of poet was that who could pronounce
now in this way, now in that ?   These are all very
reasonable questions, and as they raise very important points about an important matter—the nature
and character of Standard Spoken English—some
answer must be attempted.   The first general answer
is that the Standard of Queen Elizabeth's day, as
of Queen Anne's, was very different from that of our
own, not only in respect of details of external character, but it was far less fixed and definitely constituted.   At the present time it is possible to say in
regard to most words: Such a pronunciation will
pass muster in the best society; such another will
not, it is vulgar, either from being too precise, or
from not being precise enough; it is too pedantic,
or too slipshod; that particular type won't do outside
a given provincial area, or beyond the limits of a
certain social grade.

It was not possible to speak as categorically as
this any time from Chaucer's day to that of Pope.

A cursory study of Elizabethan English, as
exhibited in works of pure literature, reveals

considerable differences from the language of our
own day in such important features as grammatical
forms, and also, for those who know how to interpret
the spelling, in pronunciation. In the following
century a more searching examination is required
to detect marked differences in grammatical usage,
and the spelling, in printed books, becomes more
uniform, and therefore tells us less than in the preceding age. On the other hand, a far truer picture
of the English which men spoke, is derived from
hastily, and, as one may say, carelessly written,
private letters and diaries of the kind mentioned on
pp. 19, 20. If this is true for the sixteenth century, it
is still more so for the seventeenth, when the printers
show less and less variety of spelling, and when the
grammatical forms of the literary language have
become pretty well fixed. In the private documents,
however, the phonetic spellings continue, and the
grammatical forms used by quite well-educated
people, and people who frequented the best society
of their day, show a far greater variety than at
present, and include many that we should now consider as ' ungrammatical.' It is certain that the
literary prose works of the sixteenth and seventeenth
centuries give a misleading impression of the actual
spoken English of the time, and that this can only be
corrected by a study of the private documents.
In these we find, not only, as we might expect,
marked differences from our own usage, but also
considerable variety, and this among the letter-
writers who belong to the same social grade, and
who have enjoyed the same kind of education. This
diversity is very largely hidden by the more or less

dard of our own day. It was not, it could not be, a reproach to speak with a strong tinge of the dialect of one's home county. This indeed was tolerated among gentlemen. The thing to be avoided was a suspicion of citizens' English. A man might stand before kings and not be ashamed to speak with the rustic accents customary on his own estate; but he must not speak like a London shopkeeper. There are probably country gentlemen still alive, gentlemen who could never be mistaken for anything but what they are, whose speech is very powerfully modified by the dialect of their native counties. There certainly were many such within living memory. Such also we may imagine were Thomas Sackville, Waller, Dryden, John Evelyn, and a host of other writers and courtiers.

It is hard to believe that Shakespeare retained no traces of his native Warwickshire in his pronunciation. It is quite possible that the rhyme *dally–folly* discussed on p. 72, where we have to assume the pronunciation *fally*, may be an example of this, though, as is shown, *ă* for *ŏ* was coming into London speech as early as the middle of the sixteenth century (see examples *loc. cit.*).

A minute investigation of the rhymes of the early poets from the point of view of Regional dialect would probably reveal distinct evidence that many of them used forms belonging to the speech of their original home. Waller and Dryden apparently pronounced ' *beeld* ' for *build*, a form which is otherwise authenticated (*cf.* p. 103), and which would normally be attributed to the South-Eastern dialects, but may be capable of a different explanation in

other dialects; at any rate it does not appear to
have been the typical form of the ' best ' London
speech of their day.   We should expect to find that
in most cases, as with ' *beeld* ' and ' *fally*,' that
dialectal forms occurring in poetry would be disguised
beneath the conventional spelling.   In the unstudied spelling of the private letters and diaries,
however, they are often as clearly expressed as in
the dialectal texts of Middle English.   These private
documents ought to be very carefully investigated
so as to discover to what extent the Regional
dialect was current in the speech of the upper
classes in the sixteenth and seventeenth centuries
so far as this can be traced.

But we must bear in mind that even when a
definitely dialectal form is identified and located, it
is impossible, unless it be from a very remote area,
to say that it was not current among a large number
of speakers who frequented London, and even the
Court circles.   The speech of London, which, during
the fifteenth and sixteenth centuries, became more
and more the basis of the Standard, is essentially
South-East Midland in character, and this element
becomes increasingly predominant.   But while
South-East Midland is the basis of Standard English,
all sorts of other elements are grafted upon it;
sometimes in the shape of isolated words whose
form belongs to a different and remoter area;
sometimes a whole group of words belonging to a
particular Regional type, as, for example, the *ă* for *ŏ*
type in *stap* for *stop*, etc. (see discussion on pp. 71–73).
Some of these graftings have remained in Standard
English to the present day, others have disappeared.

It is such considerations as these which compel
students of the history of English to recognise that
until somewhere near the beginning of the eighteenth
century the constituent Regional elements which
composed the Standard Language were, to some
extent, in a fluid state, not definitely fixed as in
later times. The South-East Midland basis has
remained since Chaucer, but for several centuries
after his day the process continued of discarding
some pronunciations or grammatical forms, and
replacing them by other types. While the process
was in operation there was great latitude in the conception of what was ' correct ' and what was not,
and therefore, also, of what might pass muster in
the language of literary works, and in polite speech.
Hence the divergencies in usage which we see so
clearly in the published books of the sixteenth century, in the private documents written by persons
of the same class during this and the following century, and in the pronunciation, as shown by the
rhymes of these centuries.

But quite apart from the occurrence of provincial
forms, the familiar colloquial language of the sixteenth and seventeenth centuries, as reflected in the
private documents, abounds with features which,
according to our present standards of correctness,
are slipshod, careless, and ungrammatical. That
they were not so felt at the time when they were
written is manifest from the fact that the same
general character is found in nearly all the letters
in the collections mentioned above (p. 20), and
others of their kind. The same impression is
gathered from Swift's burlesque *Polite Conversa-*

tions. It has been said that from the study of these
letters and diaries we gain the conviction that the
writers are putting down on paper their actual
manner of speech. There is no question that this
is the real thing. A picture which bears every sign
of being faithful to nature, and which is consistent
in its general features as presented age after age
by the hundreds of independent persons whose
letters have been preserved, must represent not
merely the speech of these individuals, but that of
their contemporaries and associates. The letters
of Queen Elizabeth and those of the simple country
ladies, and their brothers and cousins, which we find
in the Verney Memoirs, all agree in possessing this
feature of extreme casualness, as we should think
it, in pronunciation, grammar, and syntax. The
reader must study the documents themselves, in
order to understand fully, how different from the
standards of ' correctness ' of to-day were those
of the ages of Shakespeare and Dryden, but a few
examples are given above, pp. 22–24, and in the
discussion of the loss and addition of consonants,
pp. 113–116 below. It cannot be supposed that
there were not some speakers who cultivated pre-
ciseness—indeed, we find traces of this in the
Grammarians, though hardly such as would satisfy
our present standards—but such persons must have
been exceptional in polite society, and the majority
of fashionable speakers would probably regard them
as eccentric pedants. Living as we do between two
and three centuries after the country gentlemen,
peers, and courtiers, and their wives, whose intimate
acquaintance we make in the Verney Memoirs,

it would be absurd for us to wish to correct their parts of speech, or to complain because their ideas of polite English differ from ours. We must take them and their language as we find them, and be thankful that it is possible to learn so much about the speech and manners of a period so remote. It would be foolish to refuse to accept the testimony of these intimate letters and to insist on our own ideas of propriety, many of which are only a few decades old, and of a rather dubious origin. When the change came towards what we call ' correctness,' but which our forefathers must at first have considered mere vulgar pedantry, it came for the most part from below. The Board Schools are carrying on, not perhaps so felicitously as their predecessors, the movement which was first seriously begun by Dr. Johnson's followers and imitators.

Opinions will differ as to the advantages of modern tendencies in English speech, but informed judgment will not read into the past, ideals which were unknown, nor regard as vulgar the speech of the sixteenth and seventeenth centuries because the men and women of that day do not conform to our own standards of excellence, standards which, as a matter of fact, no one in those centuries ever dreamed of. It is safe to suppose that Queen Elizabeth, Lady Hungerford, and the Verneys and their family circle spoke the best English of their times. If they did not, we may well ask, Among what class of speakers was something better to be heard ? The fact that some private letters are written in a style and with a spelling which is more regular is certainly no proof at all that the writers of them did not speak in exactly the same way as those of their contemporaries who wrote less carefully. It simply shows that the former read more printed books and remembered the orthodox spelling better. Just as the comparatively regular spelling of the poets often concealed, as we have seen, a pronunciation which did not accord with it, so the spelling of ordinary people who had a certain literary cultivation often conformed to the type generally used in printed books, without the writers' pronunciation being different in the slightest degree from that prevalent in their age and class.

Variants which are not Primarily of Dialectal Origin.

It has been said that some of the variant pronunciations and forms which are revealed by the rhymes of the sixteenth and seventeenth centuries are due to dialectal differences, but there are other important variants which have a different origin.

Stress.—One very fertile source of doublets or variant pronunciations of the same word in Middle English was difference of stress. An auxiliary verb, a personal pronoun, a preposition, was frequently uttered with no stress in a sentence. The vowels of these unstressed forms were differently pronounced from those in the same word when stressed or emphatic. Many of these old doublets survived into the seventeenth century. Thus *are* had two forms in Middle English—*āre* when stressed, *ăre* when unstressed—and the former, or, rather, its direct descendant, though now lost, was still used both in rhymes and in ordinary speech among educated persons, probably down to Pope's time. On this subject see fuller discussion (pp. 104–108) below.

This is one of the cases where the usage of the poets is supported by the Occasional Spellings, by the Grammarians, and by general philological considerations. The explanation of such rhymes as *are–fair* is perfectly simple so soon as the proper tests are applied; judged by our present habits of speech alone, such a rhyme must appear a mere makeshift. It is remarkable that in the case of several words which had, in Middle English, both strong or stressed, and weak or unstressed forms, we have now lost the old strong forms altogether and adopted the old weak forms in stressed positions, sometimes lengthening them as a result, and subjecting them to other changes consequent upon this (see p. 105) below.

Inflexion.—Another source of doublets in Middle English is the addition of an inflexional syllable, otherwise than in the Nominative and Accusative Singular if nouns, and, under certain syntactic conditions, if adjectives to words of one syllable whose vowel was short. The vowel in the uninflected cases of such words remained short; in the inflected cases it was lengthened. Thus the uninflected form of the adjective *black* was *blăc*, and in Middle English the inflected cases were *blāke*, etc. It makes an enormous difference in the subsequent history of a form whether the vowel in Middle English was long or short. Thus the uninflected Middle English form of the above adjective has given our present *black*, the inflected type has resulted in the family name *Blake* (see further on this point pp. 100, 101 below).

At the present time some words survive only in a form descended from the Middle English inflected

type, and others only in that sprung from the uninflected.

In studying the language of the first few centuries
after Chaucer, we may expect to find that both types
will often survive in the same word. The provincial dialects of to-day sometimes preserve a different
type in a given word from that used in Standard
English. Originally, however, all dialects must
necessarily have had both types, though they often
discarded one or the other, probably in the Middle
English period, and pronounced the vowel either
long or short, whether the word was inflected or not.

It is difficult to say why one type should survive
in some words, and another in others. In some cases
the particular selection may be due to some association which it is no longer possible to discover.

The evident survival of the doublets, at least, as
possible forms which the poets could use, thereby
increasing the facility of rhyming, is one of the many
instances of the unsettled character of Standard
English in the sixteenth and seventeenth centuries.
As will be seen (p. 101) in some cases, the form pre-
supposed by a poet's rhyme is actually recorded by
one or more of the contemporary Grammarians.

Coexistence at Same Period of Older and Younger Type of Pronunciation.

Since different generations overlap, and father,
son, and grandson may not only all be alive at the
same time, but may all be effective members of the
community, it follows that at a given time there
will be represented, in the same family, the slightly
different speech habits of at least three successive

generations.   The number of generations may sometimes be greater.   Now while, as a rule, a man's
mode of speech will not change much after he has
reached middle life, it is also true that a certain
amount of unconscious influence is gradually
exerted upon nearly everyone by younger speakers.
It may happen, too, that a man, so to speak, revises
his speech deliberately, in some particulars, lest it
should appear old-fashioned.   He adopts this or
that phrase or word from current slang; he weeds
out certain outworn pronunciations, and generally
brings his colloquial speech more into harmony with
that of the rising, more active generation.   But such
a process of rejuvenation, even when it is deliberate,
is never complete; the Ethiopian cannot altogether
change his skin; the leopard will retain a spot or
two.   The kind of influence which the speech of the
older generation may undergo from the younger
will hardly be in the nature of that which shows
gradual phonetic change in pronunciation.   This is
too slow to be perceptible in the course of a few
generations.   What may much more easily happen
is that when the younger speakers have adopted a
completely different type of pronunciation in certain
words, the older ones may discard their former type
and use that in vogue among their children and
grandchildren.   Thus, at the beginning of the
eighteenth century it is tolerably certain that the
majority of good English speakers pronounced
heat as *hate*, *seat* as *sate*, and so on.   Before the
death of Pope it is most probable that an increasing
number of the younger generation pronounced these
words as we do.   Dr. Johnson, for instance, evidently

Swift and Pope, though perhaps the greater proportion of certain kinds of rhymes in the works of the
former should, in most cases, be ascribed rather to
his having lived so much in Ireland, than to his comparatively slight seniority in age. As a matter of
fact, Swift is less conservative than Pope in some
things, as may be seen from the large number of
rhymes such as *morning–warning* (*cf.* pp. 69, 70).

We now bring our general survey of the problem
to a close. It has been attempted here to show
that haphazard guessing, unsupported by the kind
of knowledge requisite, does not help us to form a
sound judgment of the rhymes of the old poets,
but that the question must be tackled in a systematic manner. The various sources from which
information may be derived are indicated and
briefly described.

The chapters which follow illustrate the principles
here laid down, and the application of them to
problems arising in connection both with whole
categories of words, and with isolated forms.

The examples of rhymes do not profess to be ex-
haustive, nor is the material to which appeal is made
to illustrate the pronunciation of the sixteenth and
seventeenth centuries by any means complete.
The studious reader will, it is hoped, be sufficiently
interested to collect further illustrations of all kinds
for himself. Enough is perhaps done for him here
to convince him of the general soundness of the
methods adopted, and to show how other difficulties
not dealt with in this little work may be grappled
with, and, possibly, solved.

But when all is said and done, much more still

CHAPTER II

VOWEL QUALITY

Rhymes Based on a Vowel Quality Different from that of To-day.

THE problems dealt with in this chapter relate primarily to differences in the actual nature and character of the vowels in certain words used as rhymes. Many words were pronounced with quite a different vowel sound between the fifteenth and early eighteenth centuries from that with which the same words are pronounced now. Hence the apparent strangeness in many rhymes commonly used by the older poets. The differences we are about to consider are of such a nature as those between the vowel sound in *heat* and that in *hate*; between that in *book* and that in *brood*; between the two last and that in *flood*; between that in *join* and that in *pine*; and so on. It is true that some of these differences, as that between *brood* and *flood*, are quantitative as well as qualitative, but the latter difference is the more striking. The difference between the vowels in *book* and *brood* is mainly, though entirely, quantitative, but for historical reasons it is more convenient to consider it in this chapter. Changes in quantity often bring changes in quality of vowel sound along with them, and it is not possible to keep the two things absolutely separate.

47

Rhymes of 'Speak' with 'Make,' etc.; of 'Sea' with 'Way,' etc.

There were in M.E.—*e.g.*, in Chaucer's pronunciation—two long vowel sounds which were often spelt alike—*e, ee*. One had a sound which must have been identical with that expressed by Modern French *é*, as in *dé*. It is convenient to call this $\bar{e}^1$.

The other vowel was pronounced like modern French *ê*, as in *bête*, etc. It will be convenient to call this $\bar{e}^2$.

These two sounds can be shown to have been different from the earliest records of English speech; they are distinguished in M.E. by careful poets, such as Chaucer, who does not rhyme words containing $\bar{e}^1$ with others containing $\bar{e}^2$.

The two sounds are still distinguished by the sixteenth and seventeenth century Grammarians, and by the great majority of the best poets down to far on into the eighteenth century.

At the present day, in Standard English, words of both groups are pronounced alike with the exception of *great, steak*, and *break*, which are still pronounced with approximately their old sound.

The sound that we call $\bar{e}^1$—that is, one which, in M.E., was identical with French *é*, developed quite early its present pronunciation—that is, the sound now heard in *sweet*; this stage was certainly reached by the first half of the fifteenth century and, in some areas, probably considerably earlier.

On the other hand, $\bar{e}^2$—that is, the vowel which, in M.E., was pronounced like French *ê*—was moved on to the sound of French *é*, and there remained.

In the speech of the great majority of Englishmen, including the Standard English of the day, during the sixteenth, seventeenth, and well into the eighteenth centuries, the greater number of words containing $\bar{e}^2$ were pronounced with a sound very like French *é*, though it gradually became that which we now pronounce in *break*, etc.

Since to enumerate the various respective O.E. sources of the two sounds would involve going deeper into the history of English than the scope of this work permits, it will be convenient to the reader to give lists of typical words belonging to each group.

A. Examples of Words Originally Containing $\bar{e}^1$.

Be, been, beef, beseech, creep, deep, deer, dear, evil, feel, free, greet, hear, here, heed, he, keep, keel, keen, meek, meet, peep, queen, reel, see, seek, seem, seen, sleep, sleek, teem.

B. Words Originally Containing $\bar{e}^2$.

Beacon, bead, beam, bean, beast, bereave, beat, bequeath, bleach, breathe, bread, break, cease, cheap, clean, cream, creature, deal, defeat (noun and verb), *dread, dream, eke, eat, ease, feast, great, heal, heat, heap, heath, leaf, leap, lean* (verb), *leave, least, mead, meal, meat, peace, reach, retreat, repeat, sea, seat, sheaf, sheath, speak, squeak, steal, steak, stream, teach, veal, wreak, weave, wheat, yeast.*

In addition to these words, group B in M.E. contained a number of words such as *head, dead, death*, etc., which are now pronounced with a shortened vowel. They will be discussed later (pp. 86–90), and we shall see that in the sixteenth and seventeenth centuries, at any rate, these words were by many still pronounced with a long vowel.

We may take it as certain that all the words in group A have been pronounced, during the whole period with which we are concerned, as they are at present, while those of group B were pronounced with a vowel like French *é*.

During the sixteenth and seventeenth centuries, and part of the eighteenth, the group B words had precisely the same vowel sound as two other groups of words: (1) those which, in M.E., had *ā* (then pronounced like long Italian *a*), such as *take, name, hate, state, mate*, etc.; and (2) those still spelt with *ei, ai, ey, ay*, such as *rain, maid, convey*, etc.

If this is so, then such rhymes as *state* and *seat*, *way* and *sea* were perfect rhymes, since the B group and the other two groups just mentioned all had the same vowel sound—namely, that of French *é*— whence our present sound in *state* and *way* has developed. What has happened is that the vowel in the B group has, with the exception of that in *break, great*, and *steak*, come to be pronounced quite differently; hence the words of this group no longer rhyme with the words spelt with *a, ai, ay*, etc., but do rhyme with words of the A group above.

We have now to inquire into the reason of this. It may well be asked how it is if such words as *mead, made, maid* were all pronounced alike in the sixteenth century and later, that they are not still so pronounced. If *mead* has changed its pronunciation, why not the other two words? Or, on the other hand, if it be normal for *made* and *maid* to retain their old sound, why has *mead* undergone a change?

The Change in the Pronunciation of the Vowel in Group B Words.

That M.E. $\bar{e}^2$ in the B words lagged far behind M.E. $\bar{e}^1$ in the A words in acquiring its present sound is abundantly proved, as we shall see, by all the means of information at our disposal—the testimony of the Grammarians, the evidence of the Occasional Spellings, and the usage of the poets.

On the other hand, these sources of information also show that, side by side with the more usual pronunciation, as early as the sixteenth century, another **type** had developed among some sections of the community.   While, so far as we can judge, the vast majority of educated speakers pronounced *heat* exactly like *hate*, there were some speakers, as early as the sixteenth century, who pronounced it, and therefore, presumably, all the other words in the B group, as we pronounce them now.

The two pronunciations coexisted for centuries—we may say, if we please, that they were characteristic of different dialects—and while for a long time the old pronunciation of the B words was the more usual in polite society, the other type gradually won the day; first one word and then another came to be pronounced according to the type **we** now use, until at last, probably before the end of the eighteenth century, most educated speakers had adopted this type of pronunciation for all the words in the group, apart from the three exceptions already mentioned, and even about *great* and *break* there was some hesitation, and some eighteenth-century speakers pronounced these as ' *greet* ' and ' *breek*.'

What has happened, then, is not that the vowel in *heat*, *seat*, etc., has undergone a gradual process of phonetic change since the sixteenth century, but that one type of pronunciation has been superseded by another in the words of a whole group.

The difficulty already referred to, that *made* and *maid* and all other words containing the same vowels have not been included in the change, must be faced. There are two explanations possible. One is that, although in that dialect in which, during the sixteenth century, the vowel of the B group became identical with that of A—namely, *é*—the vowels in the *ā* and *ai* words may have undergone the same change, as indeed they must have done had all three vowels become *é* in that dialect prior to the change of this sound to that of our present ' *ee* '; nevertheless, the great difference in the spelling may have prevented the adoption by Standard English speakers of the new type for *name*, *rain*, etc., at the time when they were gradually accepting this type for the B words, which were then nearly all spelt *ea*. There is, as a matter of fact, some slight indication that *ā* was pronounced as ' *ee* ' by some speakers, though I have no evidence about the *ai*, *ay*, *ey* group.

On the other hand, it is quite possible that, in that dialect where the B words received the ' *ee* ' sound, the vowels of the other two groups had not caught them up before the change, and that the ' *é* ' stage, in *name*, *rain*, etc., was only reached later if at all. I am inclined to think that this is the true reason for the apparent inconsistency. We must remember that Standard English is not, in origin, a single uniform dialect, but a blend of several. It does not follow that, because Standard English at a given date had levelled three originally different sounds under one, all other dialects—even those nearest to London, which may have influenced the standard—had also levelled the same sounds in the same way. Indeed, we know that many Regional dialects to-day often preserve old distinctions of vowel sounds which Standard English has long abolished.

Examples of ē² Rhyming with Old ā, and ai, ei, ay, etc.

In the following lists, in order to avoid excessive subdivision, both kinds of rhymes are put together —those such as *speak* and *take* and those such as *sea* and *way*. The evidence of identity of sound between M.E. *ā*, M.E. *ai*, *ei*, and M.E. *ē²* will be produced after the examples.

Surrey, *ease–misease–please–days*. Grimald, *sea–obey*. Sackville, *break–betake, dispair–fear*; *speake–make*. Spenser, *uncleane–mayntayne*; *feature–nature–stature*. Shakespeare, *tears* (noun)*–hairs*; *nature–defeature*. Drayton, *dreams–Tames*; *raise–seize*; *plait–neat* (animal); *mead–braid*; *streight–height*; *maids–beads*; *great–wheat*; *sea–lay*; *rais'd–ceas'd*; *disdain–mean*. Habington, *sea–play, way, may, sway, away, obey, day*; *leave–crave*; *seiz'd–rais'd*; *great–state*; *beames–streames–Thames*. Suckling, *clean–Seine*. Waller, *sea–way, prey, day*; *make–snake–speak*; *fair–rear*. Cowley, *slays–please*; *plays–seas*; *ease–paraphrase*; *play–sea*; *Thames–streams*; *make–speak*. Dryden, *dream–shame*; *theme–shame* (*Absalom and Achitophel*, part ii., 369-370); *obey–sea*; *sea–lay*, *way*; *seas–displays*; *seas–sways*; *keys–obeys*. Swift, *speak–awake* ; *sea–obey* ; *lease–case* ; *seat–weight* ; *delays–peace*; *dreams–streams–Thames*; *ease–praise*; *lean–wain–clean*; *veal–ale*; *deal–fail*; *favour–beaver*; *cheap–rape*; *creature–nature*; *break–undertake*; *placed–ceased*; *dream–name*; *speake–mistake*; *ease–chaise*; *phrase are–Cæsar*; *complete–hate*; *reigns–deans*; *sea–prey, they, obey, way*; *plain–mean*; *weavers–savers*; *survey–tea* ; *please–stays* ; *yeast–haste* ; *peace–case*; *weight–seat*; *meat–say't*; *meals–fails*; *great–tête à tête* ; *plaice–peace–cease* ; *shade–mead* ; *H–teach* ; *aiding–reading*. Pope, *weak–take*; *eat–gate*; *eat–state*; *speak–take* ; *peace–race* ; *great–state* ; *race–Lucrece*; *great–rate*; *shade–dead* ; *great–cheat*.

Evidence of the Early Identity of the Vowels Expressed by a and ai, etc.

The development of old *ā* and old *ai*, as in *made* and *maid* respectively, into one and the same sound can be established as early as the fifteenth century, and the evidence becomes more plentiful later on. A few examples will suffice here of spellings which point to a levelling of the vowels. The verb 'made' is written *maid* in Coventry Leet Book in 1441; Margaret Beaufort, in 1443, writes *sa* for 'say'; *saive* for ' save ' occurs in State Papers of Henry VIII., 1515; Anne Boleyn writes *panes* for ' pains ' in 1528; *spayke* for ' spake ' and *bayde* for ' bade ' occurs in a letter of T. Pery, 1539; and Queen Elizabeth writes *maik* for ' make ' and *maid* for ' made ' in 1593.

From these spellings we may conclude that M.E. *ā* and M.E. *ai* were pronounced alike, at any rate from 1421 onwards.

In 1685 Cooper states that the pairs *made–maid*, *pain–pane*, *tail–tale* were pronounced alike.

What was this common sound ?

Early Identity of Pronunciation of M.E. ā and M.E. ē².

Bokenam, 1441, writes *credyll* for M.E. *crādel*, ' cradle,' and uses *a* for the *ē* sound, writing *bare* for M.E. *bēr*, ' bier '; in the late fifteenth-century letters of the Cely family *teke* is written for *take* and *ceme* for *came*; in Spenser's *Faerie Queen* (i. 8, 12) *retrate* is written for *retreat* and rhymed with *late*; in the Verney Memoirs, in a letter of 1655, *discrate* is written for *discreet*; and in one of 1693 *to spake* is written for *to speak*.

The evidence of the writers on pronunciation is equally conclusive. The French Grammarians of the sixteenth century compare English *ā* to French *ê, é*, and *ai*.

Wallis, in 1653, says that English *ea* and *ei* in *steal, seat, beast, receive*, etc., have the ' clear *e* ' sound of French *é*. Cooper, perhaps the best of all describers of pronunciation, says, in 1685, that *praise, convey* have the same vowel as *cane*; and also, quite definitely, that *ai* and *a* have the same sound. He also says that *meat* and *mate* are pronounced alike. His long list of words spelt then, as now, with *ea*, to which he attributes the same sound as that of ' long *a*,' contains all the words which we find in the poets rhyming with others spelt with *ā, ay, ei*, etc.

Thus the testimony of the Occasional Spellings and that of the Grammarians agree, and both are in accord with the usage of the poets.

It may seem surprising that the type of rhymes we have been considering are not commoner in the poets of the sixteenth, seventeenth, and early eighteenth centuries. Some poets, such as Milton, appear to avoid them altogether. The reason for this and for the comparative rarity in any poet except Swift may be accounted for by the poets' dislike of rhyming words together which were utterly unlike in spelling, however perfect the rhyme might be to the ear. This repugnance seems to have been especially strong in the sixteenth century, when Spenser actually often adopts a quite unhistorical spelling—*e.g.*, in *whight, bight* for *white, bite*, when he wishes to rhyme them with *right, fight*, etc. The rhyme was perfect to the ear, but it was thought desirable to make it appeal to the eye also. On this we may compare the passage in Puttenham's *Arte of English Poesie*, 1589, pp. 94-95 (Arber's Reprint). " There can not be in a maker a fowler fault, then to falsifie his accent to serue his cadence, or by untrue orthographie to wrench his words to helpe his rime, for it is a signe that such a maker is not copious in his owne language, or (as they are wont to say) not halfe his crafts maister, as for example, if one should rime to this word *Restore* he may not match him with *Doore* or *Poore* for neither of both are of like terminant, either by good orthography or in natural sound, therefore such rime is strained, so is it to this word *Ram* to say *came*, or to *Beane Den* for they sound not nor be written alike, and many other like cadences which were superfluous to recite, and are usual with rude rimers who obserue not precisely the rules of prosodie,

neuertheless in all such cases (if necessitie con-
straineth) it is somewhat more tollerable to help
the rime by false orthographie, then to leaue an
unpleasant dissonance to the eare, by keeping
trewe orthographie and loosing the rime, as for
example it is better to rime *Dore* with *Restore*
then in his truer orthographie which is *Doore* and
to this word *Desire* to say *Fier* then fyre though it
be otherwise better written *fire*."

The idea that a bad rhyme can be made less bad
by altering the spelling of one of the rhyming words
is indeed a strange one, but the passage shows that
Puttenham attached importance to ' eye-rhymes,'
and his contemporaries among the poets appear to
have shared his views.   This is the more remarkable
seeing the fluctuating habits of spelling at the time,
not only in private letters, but even in printed books.

Thus, although *seat–state*, *sea–play*, etc., were
perfect rhymes throughout the sixteenth century,
they differed so much in the usual orthography,
that poets apparently avoided them unless ' con-
strained by necessity.'

It may be worth mentioning here that after the
middle of the sixteenth century it became increas-
ingly the custom to spell $\bar{e}^1$ with *ee*, and $\bar{e}^2$ with *ea*, a
habit which has been retained in our present-day
spelling.   We may take it that when a seventeenth-
century writer speaks of the ' *ee* ' sound, he means
the sound which we now have in *see*; when he speaks
of the ' *ea* ' sound he means that which we now have
in *mate* and which he had also in *meat*.

Rhyming of ē² with ē¹.

These rhymes, which are perfect and normal now, were very rare before the eighteenth century. We have stated, and shall prove later on, that among certain speakers the vowel in the words of group B above was pronounced as at present—as ' *ee* ' as early as the sixteenth century. Those who adopted this type of pronunciation for certain words of group B could rhyme them with words from the A group —*e.g.*, *sea* with *be*, *great* with *sweet*, *stream* with *seem*, and so on. It must be mentioned at once that the vowels in the words of group B are not all of the same O.E. origin. Some of them had the sound of French *ê* in all dialects of the South and Midlands in M.E. Others, in some dialects, were pronounced with the other *ē* sound; that of French *é* in some dialects of M.E. Now, although the bulk of the rhymes (including those of Chaucer), the spellings, and the statements of the Grammarians all go to show that in the London dialect, which was the basis of Standard English, the pronunciation attributed here to the vowel in the B words was the prevailing type for all the words included in this group, even in those words whose vowel was differently pronounced in some dialects, in spite of all this, it is always possible that this or that poet may have been using the other M.E. dialectal type, which had already developed the ' *ee* ' sound at the same time that the vowel in the A words reached the ' *ee* ' stage. From the point of view of certain M.E. dialects, in fact, some of the words included above in group B belonged to group A. Thus we have

to be careful in attributing the new type of pronunciation of the genuine B ($\bar{e}^2$) words (*cf.* p. 49) to
poets of the sixteenth and seventeenth centuries;
and we can draw a certain conclusion on this point
only when the word which apparently belongs to
group B and which rhymes with one from group A
is of a class which admits of no doubt as regards its
pronunciation, because the vowel had, in M.E., the
sound of French *ê* in all dialects, and that of French
é in none.

1. The following are among the words which
belong to this category and had the *ê* sound in all
M.E. dialects in M.E.: *bead, beam, bean, beat,
bequeath, bereave, bread, break, dead, death, deaf, dream,
eke, eat, great, cheap, heap, leap, leaf, leave* (noun),
meat, speak, steal, steak, stream, weave; and the words
of French origin: *beast, defeat, ease, feast, cream,
creature, cease, peace, retreat, repeat, veal.*

2. The words which are open to doubt, and which
may possibly have been pronounced by some of the
poets, according to the ' ee ' type derived from M.E.
$\bar{e}^1$ are: *breathe, breath* (often long; *cf.* p. 88, etc.), *deal*
(verb and noun), *dread, heal, clean, heat, heath,
leave, mead, reach, sea, seat, teach, wheat.*

Rhymes of Words having Normally M.E. $\bar{e}^2$ with $\bar{e}^1$.

1. In the following lists the ' *ee*,' $\bar{e}^1$ words are
italicized.

2. The $\bar{e}^2$ words, which in some dialects had the
sound of $\bar{e}^1$ in M.E., are starred; the unstarred,
unitalicized words belong to the classes which had
$\bar{e}^2$ (*ê*) in all M.E. dialects in the South.

Wyatt, *beseech*–*reach; *spede*–*drede*–*dēde. **Surrey,** *grene*–*cleane; *reach–*beseech*. **Sackville,** *dread–*need*. **Spenser,** *seas–*these*; streeme–*seeme*; *cleene–*beene* (past participle); *uncleane–*weene*–*beseem–beene*. **Shakespeare,** *beseech* thee–*teach thee; *bleeds–proceeds*–*sheds (*cf.* also p. 89). **Marston,** *sweetness*–greatness. **Drayton,** *fleet* (n.)–beat; *these*–*seas. **Waller,** *sea–*see*; *she*–*sea; *sea–*be*. **Milton,** *sea–*thee*; *seas–*these*–seize–please. **Cowley,** *weed*–*exceed*–*read; *sea–*be*; *he*–*sea (twice); *thee*–*sea; cease–*these*. **Dryden,** *sea–*free*; *meet*–*seat; *these*–ease; bread–*feed*; *be*–*sea; plead–*freed*. **Swift,** great–*meet*; cheap–*meet*; *seas–*these*. **Pope,** *see*–flea; ease–*these*; *seat–*fleet*; *succeeds*–*spreads; *queens*–*means.

The list, even if we allow all the doubtful words to stand, is a small one; if we eliminate the starred words there is very little left. I have starred all the words belonging to the ambiguous groups because there is just the possibility of the survival of the dialect ' *ee* ' type in these. On the other hand, seeing what we know of the habitual pronunciation of all of them down to the eighteenth century, it may be thought unnecessarily fussy to cast any doubt upon them. The fact that *ea* is the traditional spelling is further proof that the B group were all normally pronounced with *é* (*ē*) and not with ' *ee* ' (*ī*).

In the above list, Spenser's rhyme *streeme–seeme*, Marston's *greatness–sweetness*, Drayton's *beat–fleet*, Habington's *disease–these*, Dryden's *bread–feed*, *plead–freed*, Swift's *great–meet*, *cheap–meet*, and Pope's *see–flea* appear to be unquestionable examples of the adoption of the new type, ' *ee*,' in old *ē²* words.

Occasional Spellings showing New Type in Old $\bar{e}^2$ Words.

The early existence of this type of pronunciation is proved by the occurrence of Occasional Spellings with *i* or *y* in words of the B group.

Machyn, 1550, has *prych*, ' preach '; *brykyng*, ' breaking '; *spykyng*. Ascham (' Toxophilus '), *lipe*, ' leap.' Gabriel Harvey, in his letters, 1573-1580, *birive*, ' bereave.' Queen Elizabeth, *bequived*, ' bequeathed,' in her Translations; and also *spike*, ' speak ' (verb).

The Grammarian Gill, in his *Logonomia*, 1621, mentions, though with strong disapproval, pronunciations of *leave* (noun) and *meat*, which he writes *liv* and *mit* respectively.

The Disappearance of the Old Type.

The old pronunciation, apart from the three words several times referred to, and from $\bar{e}$ in words where $\bar{e}^2$ stands before *r* (*cf.* p. 63, etc.), has now vanished except in some provincial dialects, notably in Irish-English, which has preserved much that is typical of the seventeenth and eighteenth centuries. The ' *ee* ' ($\bar{\imath}$) pronunciation of the group B words seems to have gained ground in the Standard Language rather slowly during the seventeenth century, and much more rapidly during the eighteenth. Already in 1701 Jones mentions *steam, team, bean, yeast* as having ' *ee*.'

In his *Plan of a Dictionary*, 1747, Dr. Johnson quotes Rowe's couplet:

As if misfortune made the throne her seat
And none could be unhappy but the great,

to illustrate the pronunciation '*greet*' for the last word, and Pope's:

> For Swift and him despised the farce of state,
> The sober follies of the wise and great,

to illustrate the other and commoner pronunciation '*grate*.'

As a matter of fact Rowe (1673-1718), undoubtedly intended *great* to be pronounced as it is now, and *seat* in the old way so as to rhyme perfectly with it. That Johnson could make this mistake shows that he assumed '*seet*' as the pronunciation of *seat*, and that this pronunciation, in this word at least, was the current one by 1747 among persons of Johnson's generation. It is certain that the new pronunciation came in gradually, and spread to one word of the group after another. Cowper, in a well-known hymn, still rhymes *sea* with *way*. This may, however, be a traditional rhyme so far as he is concerned. The old pronunciation no doubt survived in the provinces, even among highly educated speakers, much later than in London. In this connection it is interesting to note that Charles Lloyd, the Quaker banker of Birmingham (1748-1828), who published translations of Homer and Horace, writes: 'Christopher Wordsworth is too nice about rhymes; he thinks "*steall*" and "*prevail*" do not quite suit. I believe Londoners pronounce *steal steel*, but we pronounce it *stale*.' (Cf. *Charles Lamb and the Lloyds*, E. V. Lucas p. 206.)

M.E. ê¹ and ē² before -r.

The rhymes of the early poets which are based on words such as *bear* (verb), *hear*, *fear*, *ear*, etc., appear to exhibit a remarkable diversity of usage, whether we compare them with our own pronunciation of these words, or consider the M.E. origin of the vowels. It is not easy to see light in this question. As regards present-day standard it seems to be the case that a much smaller number of words containing $\bar{e}^2$ before -*r* are pronounced according to the ' *ee* ' type than of those with the same original vowel before other consonants. It is particularly important in dealing with this problem to distinguish between the *sound* and the official *spelling*, because the latter is by no means consistent, *ea* being sometimes written to express both the sound in *tear* (verb) and *tear* (from the eye). As a proper phonetic notation is here ruled out we had better distinguish the two vowels involved in this discussion as ' *ea* ' and ' *ee* ' respectively, after the manner of the seventeenth-century Grammarians, using ' *ea* ' when speaking of the sound in the verb *tear*, etc., and ' *ee* ' for the sound in *tear* from the eye, etc.

A. ' ea ' Words.—(*a*) The following words, now pronounced with ' *ea*,' had originally $\bar{e}^2$ in all M.E. Southern dialects, and the sound has been but little changed: *bear* (verb, and name of animal), *tear* (verb), *swear*, *wear* (verb).

(*b*) The following had usually $\bar{e}^2$ in the London dialect, but were pronounced with $\bar{e}^1$ in several neighbouring dialects: *there*, *were*, *where*, *hair*, *ere*.

B. ' ee ' Words.—(*a*) The following, now pronounced with ' *ee*,' had $\bar{e}^1$ in M.E.: *here, hear, dear, deer, leer* (verb), *dreary, beer, weary*.

(*b*) The following had $\bar{e}^2$ in some dialects and $\bar{e}^1$ in others, so that the present form may be from the latter type: *bier, fear, rear* (verb), *year*.

(*c*) The following had $\bar{e}^2$ in all M.E. dialects: *tear* (from the eye), *spear, shear* (verb), *ear* (noun, organ of hearing; of grain; and verb = ' plough '), *beard, smear* (verb).

It is apparent from these examples that there is not perfect consistency in our present usage in the development of the same sound. Groups A (*b*) and B (*b*) had originally the same vowel, one which might, in M.E., be either $\bar{e}^1$ or $\bar{e}^2$, yet we now pronounce them differently. If it be normal for the sound of $\bar{e}^2$ to remain before -*r*, why has it not remained in both of these groups ? If Standard English selected the $\bar{e}^1$ type in group B (*b*), why not in the other group also ? Again, in group B (*c*) all the words are undoubted $\bar{e}^2$ words, yet they have a different pronunciation to-day from the other, equally certain $\bar{e}^2$ words in A (*a*).

If the former have developed the ' *ee* ' sound, the latter might have done so equally well. We are apparently confronted with another instance of two streaks of different dialectal influence in our present Standard. One dialect strain apparently did not develop old $\bar{e}^2$ into ' *ee* ' before -*r*, while the other did.

In the case of A (*b*) and B (*b*) there is further complication, since there is the possibility of different dialect types surviving from M.E.

The inconsistencies in the rhymes of the old poets are due to the same causes as those which exist in our own speech, only we cannot discover the latter unless we regard the historical development of the forms and their origin.

The same divergencies are found to-day in the provincial dialects; they appear in the statements of the old Grammarians, and in the rhymes of the old poets. If there appears greater confusion in the forms of the *ear* or *eer* words in the old rhymes than at the present day, such diversity of usage must be put down to the unsettled state of the Standard in the sixteenth and seventeenth centuries, due to the causes mentioned on pp. 31–42 above.

A few examples will show how the early Grammarians reflect the divergent usage: *Beard,* ' *ea* ' Cooper and Jones; *cheerful,* with ' *ea* ' Gill and Hodges; *dear,* ' *ee* ' Smith and Gill, the latter also ' *ea* '; Butler ' *ea,* ' expressing disapproval of ' *ee* ' type; *ear,* ' *ea* ' Gill and Butler, who considers the ' *ee* ' type ' corrupt '; *fear,* ' *ea* ' Gill, ' *ee* ' Cooper; *hear,* ' *ea* ' Butler, who says ' *ee* ' is ' corrupt ' in this word; *near,* ' *ee* ' Smith and Butler, ' *ea* ' Hart and Gill; *shears,* ' *ea* ' Gill, ' *ea* ' Cooper; *spear,* ' *ea* ' Gill, ' *ee* ' Cooper; *tear,* ' *ea* ' (for verb and noun) Smith; *year,* ' *ee* ' Salesbury, Bullokar, Butler, ' *ea* ' Gill; *weary,* ' *ea* ' Gill and Butler: the latter considers the ' *ee* ' type ' corrupt.'

It is not surprising that the rhymes should reflect the prevailing unsettled state of pronunciation.

Roister Doister, *beare–heare* ; Wyatt, *bear–hear,* *were–pere,* ' peer '; Sackville, *near–hear,* *there–fear,* *fear–hair,* *where–tear,* *despair–fear,* *fears–ears,* bears (verb)–*spears* ; Spenser, *beare* (verb), *pear, dear, heare–were, clear–beare, heares,* ('hairs')–*weares, were– yfere,* 'together'; Shakespeare, *swears–tears, ear– hair, fear–there, ear–there, dear–fear, here–bear–dear, wear* (verb)–*year, years–forbears* ; Drayton, *here– were, bears–ears, cares–tears, air–dear, fear–hair, peers–years*; Suckling, *appear–swear, fair–clear, fear– swear–bear* ; Donne, *there–careere, upbeare–hair, neere– deere* (adj.)–*were, ears–haires, where–fear, appears– forbears* ; Milton, *appear–bear, dear–wear, peer–bier– tear, there–cheere, drear–ear–career–appear* ; Cowley, *ear–share, prayer–here, ears–spheres, there–tear, there– declare* ; Waller, *here–bear, fear–care, ears–tears, there–here, bears–peers, year–wear, here–year, year– there, fair–rear, ear–deer* ; Dryden, *spares–tears, bear–fear, swear–fear, fear–share* ; Swift, *shares– ears, cheer–career, swears–ears, severe–air.*

As a result of this rather tedious discussion, the conclusion I am inclined to, considering the available facts, is that probably nearly all the above rhymes were good in their day—that is, the words paired together might be pronounced so as to rhyme, without eccentricity, or departure from a current usage. There was evidently great variety in the distribution of the types. It is, however, open to question whether those words which had only $\bar{e}^1$ in all M.E. dialects were ever normally pronounced with the '*ee*' sound before -*r*. The whole history of $\bar{e}^1$ and $\bar{e}^2$ before -*r* requires a special and most thorough investigation, and pending this, we shall do well to reserve our judgment. It seems certain, however, that $\bar{e}^2$ really was pronounced with '*ea*' before -*r*, in the sixteenth and seventeenth centuries, in words where we now pronounce ' *ee*,' such as *fear, ear*, etc. The modern pronunciation of the last word may have been influenced by the verb *hear*, which is so intimately associated with it in meaning.

Rhymes with Words containing the Combination wa-, wha-, qua-.

At the present time the sound expressed by the letter *a* in these combinations is a ' short *o*.' Thus, *what* rhymes perfectly with *hot, wand* with *pond, quarrel* with *sorrel*. When *r* follows the *a* (in spelling) in words of one syllable, the vowel is lengthened, so that instead of ' short *o* ' we get what may be popularly called the ' *aw* sound.' Thus *war* rhymes with *sore, quart* with *port*, and so on. If it were not for the spelling, it would never occur to anyone nowadays to think that such pairs as *hand–wand* were rhymes at all, any more than, say, that *hat* and *pot* are rhymes. Such rhymes as *hand–wand, warm–harm*, which appeal to the eye, but not at all to the ear, according to our present pronunciation, are nevertheless quite common in the sixteenth and seventeenth centuries ; in fact, we do not find, with one possible exception, any rhymes of *wa* words with others spelt with *o* until far on in the seventeenth century, when Dryden rhymes *war–abhor*.

If we believe that the poets, on the whole, use true rhymes, we might infer from this that our present pronunciation was not very widespread, certainly not universal, among the best English

speakers before Dryden's generation. This view is
strongly supported by other evidence. The facts
are these:

The writers on pronunciation down to 1640 seem
to make no mention of the ' *wo* ' pronunciation,
whether long or short. Thus, for instance, Mul-
caster, in 1583, puts *warde, dwarf, warn, warp*, etc.,
when speaking of the vowel sound, in the same list
as *cast, far, clasp*, etc. In 1640, however, Daines
says that *au*, meaning the vowel in *saw*, is pronounced in *quart, wart, swart, thwart*. Cooper
(1685) says that ' guttural *o*,' as he calls it—that is,
the ' *aw* ' sound—is expressed by *a* after *w*, and
occurs in *was, watch, war, warm, water*, etc.

The Occasional Spellings show that the new
pronunciation did exist rather earlier than the
Grammarians admit. The fifteenth-century Cely
Papers write *wosse* and *whosse*, etc., for *was*, though
this may represent an unstressed form and is not
conclusive, but Machyn (1550) writes *wosse* for *wash*,
which is. I have not found any more of these
spellings before the Verney Memoirs, which cover the
period of Daines, Cooper, and Dryden, and in these
letters there are a fair number of such spellings as
wos, ' was '; *whot*, ' what '; *wore*, ' war '; *woshing*,
' washing '; *woching*, ' watching '; *Worrik, quorrill,
quollity*, etc.

Now Machyn was a vulgar fellow, and his pronunciation was most certainly not the politest of
his day. It is safer, therefore, to believe the writers
on pronunciation of the sixteenth and early seventeenth centuries, when they state that ' short *a* '
after *w* was pronounced in the same way as other

'short *a*'s,' and to suppose that *wosh*, etc., was a vulgar or provincial pronunciation which made its way slowly among the better class of speakers. It is significant that the recognition of the new pronunciation by the Grammarians, the occurrence of any considerable number of *wo-* spellings by persons of the upper class, the rhyming of *wă-* words with others containing the *ŏ* sound, all occur during about the same period. We may conclude, then, that the rhymes of the poets during the sixteenth and the greater part of the seventeenth centuries were in accordance with the best usage of that age. They were perhaps inclined to be conservative in these as in other rhymes which involved coupling together words in which the vowel sounds, though identical, were expressed by an entirely different spelling. As the following lists show, Dryden has a far larger number of the old-fashioned rhymes than of the new, and Pope has apparently none of the latter. In Dryden's heyday the old pronunciation must still have been far commoner than in Pope's, and the rhymes of the younger poet in this respect may perhaps be regarded as merely traditional and no more genuine rhymes for most of his contemporaries than they would be at the present time.

Rhymes in Words with wa-.

Rede me, *barell–quarell*; *pas–was*; *warre–prefare*. Roister Doister, *was–masse–passe*. Wyatt, *ranne–wanne*; *warme–arm*; *warre–marre*. Surrey, *warme–arme*; *ar–warre*. Sackville, *regard–reward*; *was–glass*. Spenser, *reward–prepard*; *warre–jarre*; *regard–*

heard; *unreguarded–unrewarded*; *wan–can*; *ward–
to guard*; *what–chat*; *was–brasse*; *wannc–scanne–
swanne*; *warme–charme–farme*. **Watson** ('Teares of
France,' 1593), *swans–songs*. (This is, in any case,
no more than an assonance, but could hardly have
been used unless 'swons' had been in the poet's
mind.) **Shakespeare,** *war–jar*; *warm–harm*. **Dray-**
ton, *ran–wan*; *dashes–washes*; *warm–harm*; *far–war*;
wan–began; *pass–was*. **Donne,** *watched–catched*; *war
–are*; *swan–than*. **Habington,** *began–swan*; *are–war*;
saint–want; *warme–charme*. **Milton,** *span–scan–wan*.
Dryden, *wars–scars*; *want–grant*; *heard–reward* (see
p. 122 on pronunciation *hard*); *bar–war*; but *wallow–
follow* (Epilogue to 'Sir Fopling Flutter'); *war–abhor*
('Death of Oliver Cromwell,' 11). **Cowley,** *plant–want*.
Waller, *arm–warm*; *far–war*; *quash'd–dash'd*. **Swift,**
wan–Dan–man; *wand–hand*; *quarter–garter*; *hard–
reward*; *squabble–rabble*; *thatch–watch*; but *morals–
quarrels*; *short–quart*; *warning–morning*; *quarter–
mortar*; *brawler–Waller*; *draws–was*; *followed–
swallowed*; *Waller–smaller*; *warms–informs*; *warm'd–
perform'd*. **Pope,** *quarter–martyr*; *care–war*; *man–
swan*; *rewards–cards*; *appeared–reward* (a bad
rhyme).

Rhymes of 'Short o' with 'Short a.'

During the sixteenth and seventeenth centuries
a habit or fashion arose in Standard English of pronouncing 'short *o*' like 'short *a*' in certain words.
There are very few survivals of this to-day, and only
in words in which the spelling has helped to fix the
pronunciation, such as *Gad, egad*, which are almost
obsolete; *strap*, earlier *strop*, which also survives in

its original form with specialised meaning; *plat* of ground instead of *plot* occurs in the Authorised Version of the Old Testament.

This style of pronunciation is apparently a Westernism which penetrated in Standard and London English in the sixteenth century. It is found in the Wiltshire poem ' The Life of St. Editha' (*c.* 1420), where *starme* occurs for *storm*, and it is typical at the present time in the popular speech of the South-West and South-West Midlands of England.

Why or how this peculiarity should have passed beyond its normal regional limits we cannot tell, but the Occasional Spellings and the statements of some of the Grammarians show that it was at one time fairly widespread among all classes, and in Vanbrugh's *Relapse* it is ridiculed as a fashionable affectation prevalent among fops.

I have not noted many traces of the unrounded —that is, the *ă* forms, in rhymes, but those which do occur are noteworthy on account of.the importance of the writers in whose works they are found.

The short list is as follows:

Spenser, *plot–that* (' Death of Sir Philip Sidney'); **Shakespeare,** *dally–folly* (' Rape of Lucrece,' 554–556); **Donne,** *that–not* (this, however, may represent a survival of M.E. *nat*); **Swift,** *yonder–salamander* (' Description of a Salamander').

The following evidence makes it certain that these were perfect rhymes, and goes to show how faithfully the prevailing fashions of speech of their day are reflected in the writings of the early poets.

Machyn has the following spellings, amongst

others, which evidently express the unrounded forms:
caffen, ' coffin '; *marrow*, ' morrow '; *hars*, ' horse ';
Dasset, ' Dorset '. Lady Hungerford (1569) writes
swarn for *sworn*; Queen Elizabeth writes *stap* for
'stop' in a letter to her cousin, James VI. of Scotland;
Gill, the purist High Master of St. Paul's School,
writes *skalers* in 1621 for ' scholars,' as a burlesque
of the affected pronunciation of his day; the letter-
writers of the Verney Memoirs write *fally* (1647),
sassages (1640), *aclake*, ' o'clock ' (1652), etc.; Mrs.
Basire (1655) writes *Gearge*, ' George.' Vanbrugh
makes his arch-fop, Lord Foppington, say *stap*,
Tam, *Gad*, *pasitively*, *bax*, ' box,' etc. Lady Wentworth (1708) writes *beyand*.

The first Grammarian to note these forms is
Bellot (1580), who says that English *ŏ* is almost like
French *ă*; a work called *Alphabet Anglois* (1625)
says of English *o* that it ' se prononce souvent come
A.' *Thames*, *chart=Thomas*, *short*. Hodges (1643)
says that *chaps–chops*, *fallow–follow*, *farmer–former*
are pronounced ' near alike.' Mauger (1679) repeats
his predecessor's statement that English *ŏ* is like
French *ă*, and gives the pronunciation *fram*, *anan*,
nar, *nat*, *Gad*, *ladge*, *frast* for the words which we
spell and pronounce with *ŏ* or its equivalent.

Thus not only is the existence of the type of pronunciation under discussion amply established from
every possible source, but the four actual words—
folly, *plot*, *not*, *yonder*—which occur in the above
short list of rhymes are all shown by collateral
evidence to have been pronounced in the manner
required to constitute perfect rhymes in the passages
referred to.

Rhymes of M.E. -i- with -oi-.

Such rhymes as *repine–join*, *smile–spoil*, etc.,
occur in the poets from the sixteenth to the eighteenth centuries, and, in spite of the difference of
sound between ' long *i* ' and *oi* at the present day,
there were good rhymes according to the English
habits of pronunciation which obtained far into the
eighteenth century.

Oi was always a diphthong, and in M.E. had
pretty much the same sound as at present. During
the period between the latter part of the fifteenth
century, however, *oi* came to be pronounced pretty
much as it is to-day in the rustic speech of Oxford-
shire—that is, a diphthong composed of the vowel
sound in *but* followed by that in *pit*. While in this
stage of development *oi* was caught up by the old
i, which in the M.E. period and before, had the
' continental ' sound as in modern French *dire*, etc.

The normal development of this diphthong in
Standard English is heard in *wine, bite, smile*, etc.,
at the present time. Since *oi* had, in the fifteenth
century, exactly the same pronunciation as old *i*,
we should expect that it would have the same pronunciation now, and the fact that it has not must be
put down to the influence of the spelling. Among
many provincial and vulgar speakers the pairs
loin and *line, boil* and *bile* are still pronounced exactly
alike. What is now a provincialism or a vulgarism
was formerly a characteristic of the best English.

The identity of the two diphthongs which have
now been separated is established from the fifteenth
century by the Occasional Spellings, confirmed

by the statements of Grammarians, and reflected in the rhymes of the old poets.

The identity is proved by *oi*, *oy* being written for *ī*, and *i* or *y* for *oi*.

The following examples of Occasional Spellings will suffice to illustrate this:

'Life of St. Editha' (1420), *anynted*, 'anointed.' Lord Mayor Gregory (*c.* 1460) has *destryde*, 'destroyed'; *pyson*, 'poison.' 'Translation of Monk of Evesham' (1482), *defoyled*, 'defiled.' 'Rede me and be not wroth' (1528), *defoyling*. Verney Memoirs, *gine*, 'join' (1656); *byled leg of mutton* (1670); *implyment*, 'employment' (1686).

From the sixteenth century the writers on pronunciation distinguish two, sometimes three, pronunciations of *oi*, namely: (1) what appears to be '*ooi*' (*ui*); (2) the combination of the sound in *but* followed by 'short *i*'; and (3) *oi* as at present. The seventeenth-century writers are the clearest on these differences. The first of these types seems to occur only after lip consonants—*e.g.*, in *boil*, *moil*, *point*, etc., and to be a variant of type (2), while the third is apparently the beginning of the present pronunciation based on the spelling. Cooper (1685) says that *wine*, *blind* have the same sound as *ointment*, *broil*, *injoin*, but seems also to suggest that some speakers use *oi* in both of groups (1) and (2). Cooper also says that *oil*, *I'll*, *isle* are all pronounced alike. Hodges (1641) says that *lines* and *loins* have the same sound. Baker (1724) says that *coin* is pronounced *quine*. Later writers insist on the restored pronunciation in some words and not in others. Thus Kendrick, 1773, says that it is an affectation to pronounce *boil, join* otherwise than as *bile, jine,* but that it is ' vicious ' to pronounce *oil, toil* as *isle* and *tile,* as is frequently done.

The following are a few examples of *oi–ī* rhymes from Spenser to Pope:

Rhymes of oi with Old ī.

Spenser, *toyle–compile–awhile–assoyle.* Shakespeare, *swine–groin* (' Venus and Adonis,' l. 1116). (This is an example of *oi* for *i*; *grine* is the original. The spelling has unaccountably survived and produced an artificial pronunciation). Habington, *repine–joyne,* l. 71, *joyn'd–shined*; *smile–spoile,* l. 87. Suckling, *smile–coil*; *sign–coin* (' Session of Poets '). Waller, *toil–isle* (' Summer Island,' l. 54). Denham, *reviles–spoils* (' Cooper's Hill,' ll. 341-2). Cowley, *entwin'd–joyn'd* (' Elegy upon Anacreon '). Dryden, *refines–joins–loins,* ll. 689-691; *join–sign* (' The Hind and the Panther,' 412-413). Swift, *surprizeon–poison.* Pope, *toil–pile* (' Lord Cobham,' l. 220); *design–coin* (' To Addison,' ll. 23-4); *join–divine* (' To Augustus,' ll. 101-2).

Rhymes with Words Spelt oo—the Three Types.

In recent times poetic usage in respect of rhyming such words as *flood* with *good,* or either of them with *food,* etc., is very lax. Again, *love* is frequently rhymed with *move,* etc. If it were not for tradition and identity of spelling it would hardly occur either to a poet or to his readers that the association of *flood* with *good* constituted a rhyme at all. As it is, owing to the identical graphic expression of totally different sounds, and to poets having accustomed

us to these ' rhymes,' the badness of them passes
unremarked. In M.E. most of the words now spelt
with *oo*, no matter which of the three sounds they
now contain, were pronounced with one and the
same vowel sound—one not very different from that
heard in German *Bohle*, etc. It was therefore natural
and proper that, down probably to the fourteenth
century, the sound being the same in *flood*, *food*, and
good, these words should be rhymed together.
Now, one original sound has developed into three
distinct sounds. Briefly stated, what has happened
is this. (1) Sometime, probably by the fourteenth
century, one of the M.E. ' long *o* ' sounds, which
we may call $\bar{o}^1$, developed into the sound now heard
in Standard English in *moon*, *doom*, and *food*. In
these and several other words of this class this long
sound has remained to this day. (2) In another large
group of them, however, the vowel was shortened
quite early—certainly during the fifteenth century—
and this sound, before the close of the century,
underwent the process known as ' unrounding,'
resulting ultimately in the vowel sound now heard
in *blood*, *flood*, *glove*, *month*, etc. Thus, in the sixteenth century, there were two sounds where, as
late as Chaucer's time probably, there had still been
but one.

(3) Later on, perhaps not till the late seventeenth
century, or even later—it is at present impossible
to be sure of the approximate date—the vowel in
a certain number of the words which had retained
the ' long *oo* ' sound (as in *moon*, etc.) underwent
a new process of shortening. It is this process which
has produced the short sound in *good*, *hood*, *stood*,

etc. Hence our three types at the present time—
the survivals of the old long vowel, *moon*, etc.; the
early shortening and unrounding, as in *gloves*, *flood*,
etc.; the late shortening, as in *good*, *stood*, etc.

In Standard English at the present day there is
no doubt according to which type any word whose
vowel is derived from M.E. $\bar{o}^1$ is pronounced. It
is impossible to explain the distribution of the three
types. We cannot even say why the vowel in some
words should have undergone the early shortening,
while that in others did not; nor why the later
shortening should affect some words but not others.
There seems to be nothing in the phonetic character
of the words involved to explain it, except that before
-*k* as in *hook*, *shook*, etc., we invariably have the
later shortening. We must conclude, therefore,
that the two shortening processes occurred only in
the speech of some sections of the community,
while among other groups of speakers one or other
of these tendencies did not obtain; in yet other groups
perhaps neither shortening took place. Present-day
standard, according to this view, reflects, in different
words of the class we are considering, the speech
habits of different varieties or dialects. Whether
these were originally Regional variants, which gained
a footing in the speech of a particular class and so
gradually found their way into the standard, or
whether they were purely Class Dialect in origin,
we cannot say.

The exact distribution of the types, which is now
so definitely fixed in Standard English, was for a
long time a fluctuating usage. The present writer
can remember hearing, in his boyhood, an old man,

a speaker who had otherwise no peculiarities or vulgarisms, pronounce *soot* so as to rhyme with *cut*. This was a survival of the type produced by the early shortening, and there is evidence, from the Grammarians, and from the Occasional Spellings, that this word was habitually so pronounced in the seventeenth century. As a rule such differences of usage as exist to-day are confined to the later shortening. *Groom, broom,* and *soon* may be heard among speakers of Standard English sometimes with a long vowel, sometimes with a short. The group of words which are pronounced with the vowel in *cut*, on the other hand, is definitely limited; no one hesitates as to which they are; their number never increases or diminishes. In the sixteenth and seventeenth centuries, however, the distribution of the two, or, towards the end of the seventeenth century, those types then existing, is by no means fixed. If we compile a list of all the $\bar{o}^1$ words whose pronunciation is described by the Grammarians of these centuries, we shall probably find authority for both pronunciations of every word. Thus in the sixteenth century *good* is represented by Salesbury (1547) and Smith (1568) as being pronounced with both a long and a short vowel, by Gill with a short vowel; *blood*, according to Smith, had a long vowel, according to Bullokar (1580) a short; *flood*, by Salesbury, with a long, by Bullokar and Gill with a short, and so on. In the seventeenth and early eighteenth century *good*, according to Price (1668), had a short vowel (that in *cut*); Jones (1701) gives the same pronunciation, but another, apparently that which we now use, as better; Cooper (1685) gives only a short vowel; for *foot* Price gives a long vowel, Cooper a short (the one we use) as the best, and another short (with the vowel in *cut*) as a barbarous pronunciation; *soot* is described by Price as having a long vowel, by Cooper with a short (same as ours) by Jones with the sound in *cut*, and also with the short vowel as at present, which he considers better. These few examples are enough to show the variety of pronunciations existing formerly in words of this class, if the Grammarians are to be trusted. We are, however, further able to collect, from scattered spellings, that the early shortening occurred in the sixteenth and seventeenth centuries in words which are now pronounced in Standard English according to a different type. Bishop Fisher writes *futt*, ' foot,' in his sermons; Gabriel Harvey in his letters writes *futt*, *whudd*, ' hood,' in a poem rhyming with *budd*; Rhoades, the Verneys' steward, writes *tuck*, ' took' (1653); and Sir Ralph Verney writes *sutt*, ' soot ' (1686). All these apparently imply a pronunciation which would result in the vowel in *cut* at the present time.

On the other hand, the spelling *ou*, which is common for the new sound developed from M.E. $\bar{o}^1$, from the fourteenth century onwards, may probably imply, when we find it in the sixteenth century, an unshortened type, and this spelling occurs occasionally in words where the present standard type is from that with early shortening. *Bloud*, ' blood,' occurs in Edward VI.'s First Prayer Book (1549), in Latimer's Sermons, in Bishop Fisher's Sermons, and Sir Thomas Smith's *De Republica Anglicana*, etc.; *floude* is found in the First Prayer Book,

This book also has the spellings *fluddes* and *bludde*, showing the early shortening as in our present type. It is quite possible, however, that *ou* was written indifferently for the long and for the shortened vowel. The long type of *flood* is suggested by Drayton's rhyme with *brood* mentioned below. Butler (1642) protests against writing *ou* in *blood*, *stood*, *courage*, etc., ' since *ou* hath another sound in *loud*, *proud*, etc., while the same sound hath another writing in *good*, *stood*, *mud*, *bud*,' etc. This seems to imply that all the above words in Butler's pronunciation, except *loud* and *proud*, had the same vowel. The introduction of *mud* and *bud* into the list proves this to have been the (early) shortened sound.

It seems a justifiable inference from the various facts cited, and many more examples might be collected to the same effect from the Grammarians, that neither the long nor the short pronunciation of any word of the old $\bar{o}^1$ class need be ruled out as possibly current during the sixteenth and seventeenth centuries. The popular dialects at the present time show great variety in the types which they use of these words. In some dialects, although the early shortening took place, the resulting vowel was not unrounded; in others the early shortening went much further than in Standard English, and was accompanied by unrounding, so that a larger number of words exist pronounced according to the *flood* type; in other dialects, again, the later shortening was far more restricted in its effects than in Standard English, so that, for instance, none of the words ending in -*k* are affected at all, and *cook*, *book*, etc., are pronounced with a long vowel; finally, there are dialects in which the late shortening has gone further than in Standard English, with the result that *food* is pronounced with the same vowel as in Standard *good*. The possibilities of Regional Dialect pronunciations obtaining currency among the best speakers from the time of Elizabeth to that of Anne are discussed on pp. 34–38 above.

All things considered, it seems more probable that the poets who, in the sixteenth and seventeenth centuries, appear to us to confuse the various types in their rhymes are, in reality, basing these upon a pronunciation according to which the agreement in sound was perfect. If this were so it would account for the formation of a tradition in virtue of which alone the later poets can hope to justify the licence of their usage. A few examples may be given from the early poets. The rhymes of *love* and *above* with *move* and *prove*, etc., are omitted. They are common in the poets and were perfectly good. There is evidence on the one hand that *prove* could be pronounced with the same vowel which we now have in *love*, and on the other that this word and *above* could be pronounced with the sound which we now have in *prove* and *move*.

Roister Doister rhymes *good–blood*; **Wyatt,** *flood–food*; **Sackville,** *withstood–blood, good–blood*; **Spenser,** *buds–woods, budde–good*; **Shakespeare,** *blood–stood, blood–good, wood–blood*; **Drayton,** *woo'd–stood, took–luck, flood–stood, flood–brood*; **Donne,** *blood–stood–good, good–stood–food*. **Suckling** has *look–struck*; **Milton,** *flood–mood, –good*, also *flood–mud*; **Dryden** has *flood–mood–good, good–blood, stood–blood, withstood–flood*.

Such rhymes as Milton's *moon–whereon*, and Dryden's *load–good*, *flood–rode*, *crowd–blood*, *understood–abroad*, and Swift's *over–lover* must be set down as imperfect in their own or any other age.

Pope's rhyme *pother–other* is justified by Jones (1701), who includes both words in the same list.

Rhymes Implying Pronunciation of ĕ for ĭ.

The habit of pronouncing *ĕ* for *ĭ* was so common among the upper classes and others during the whole of the sixteenth, the seventeenth, and the first third of the eighteenth centuries that it is rather surprising not to find more traces of it in the poets. I have noted only the following: **Spenser, Drayton, Waller, Swift,** and **Pope** all rhyme *spirit–merit*; **Spenser** has *riches–wretches*; **Dryden** repeatedly rhymes the word *prince* with such words as *sense*, *thence*, *offense*, *incontinence*, *pretence*; **Lady Mary Montagu** rhymes *wit* with *coquet* and *gift* with *theft*.

The Occasional Spellings give ample support for the view that the above words were really pronounced so as to rhyme. *Sence*, etc., ' since,' is written by Sir Thomas Elyot, Bishop Latimer (Sermons), writers in the Verney Memoirs (1645, 1652), Mrs. Basire (1651), and Lady Wentworth. Queen Elizabeth writes *rechis*, ' riches ' (*cf.* Spenser above); Lady Sussex, Verney Memoirs, writes *speriets*; and Mrs. Basire writes *Prence* (1655) (*cf.* Dryden). Many more examples might be given, but these will suffice.

Rhymes of -er- with -ar-.

The combination -er- became -ar- in the M.E. period, though the latter spellings are not very abundant before the fifteenth century. From then onwards they become increasingly frequent, and there is no evidence that the type of pronunciation represented by the spelling -ar- was characteristic of any particular Regional dialect. In standard spoken and printed English many words have become fixed both in pronunciation and spelling with -ar-: *carve, dark, far, farthing, farm, part, harvest, jar, parson,* ' clergyman,' *smart, starve,* etc. Others, such as *heart, hearth, clerk,* retain the old pronunciation but have a different spelling. There is no doubt, from the evidence of the Occasional Spellings, that down to the middle of the eighteenth century the -ar- type was far more widespread in fashionable speech than it is to-day. Most of the words whose official spelling had not been stereotyped with -ar- have had their pronunciation ' restored,' probably on account of the -er- spelling, *clerk, Derby,* and *Bertie* being almost the only exceptions. In the private letters of the sixteenth and seventeenth centuries we find a large number of -ar- spellings, and the list of these includes nearly every word which originally had -er- in M.E. We may be sure when a word is spelt -ar- which type the writer intended to express, but we cannot be certain that the same type was *not* intended when the older M.E. spelling -er- is retained.

Among the words spelt -ar- between the middle of the fifteenth and the early part of the eighteenth

century are the following, many of which occur
again and again as written, while others are rarer
in this form (the words of which several examples
occur are starred): *Clargy, *sartayne, sartin, etc.,
darth, divart, divartion, defar, consarne, confarm,
farvent, *larn, *marcy, *parson=person, prefar,
sarche, ' search ' (1515) (cf. Swift's rhyme), sarmon,
*sarve, *sarvant, *sarvis, *desarve, presarve, *swarve,
- vartu, varmin. On hard, ' heard,' cf. p. 122 below.
Many of these forms, differing from our present
usage, are mentioned also by the Grammarians.

Only a few of these rhymes have been collected to
illustrate a usage different from our own, but it
would be very easy to find many more examples.
We may safely conclude that the following rhymes
were perfectly sound:

Rede me and be not wroth, carve–serve. Wyatt,
disarne–harm; hert (heart)–convert–smart. Sackville,
apart–revert–heart. Spenser, heart–convert; pervart–
hart–start; regard–hard (heard); warre–jarre. Shakespeare, ward–regard–heard. Drayton, serv'd–starv'd.
Suckling and Cowley, serve–starve. Milton, earth–
hearth (probably -ar- type in both words; Cooper,
1685, gives harth as the pronunciation of the latter
word). Dryden, serv'd–starv'd; preferr'd–heard (probably hard type); heard–guard–reward; deserve–starve;
disperse–stars; desért–part; art–desart. Swift, verse–
stars; verse–farce–scarce; charge ye–clergy; searches–
arches, snarling–berlin (name of a carriage, named
after Berlin); deserve–starve; stars–hearse. Pope,
observe–, reserve–starve.

Note on -ure, etc., in Unstressed Syllables.

French *u* normally became *i* in unstressed syllables before most consonants—*e.g.*, in our pronunciation of *biscuit, minute, conduit*. Formerly this kind of pronunciation was almost universal (*cf. valy,* ' value,' *nevie,* ' nephew,' p. 17). Before *-n*, as in *fortune*, the same thing happened, and ' *fortin* ' was the normal pronunciation of this word, as we see from Machyn's *mvsseforten* and the frequent *fortin, fortine* in the Verney Memoirs.

Before *-r, i* became the ' murmur ' vowel, and is variously written: *moister* (*-ure*) (translation of ' Palladius,' *c.* 1420); *venter* (Cely Papers, 1480); *unscripterly* (Bishop Latimer); *venterous, ventorer* (Machyn); *ventarous, jointer* (Verney Memoirs, 1642); *creetors, torter, picturs* (Wentworth Papers). Cooper says that *picture* is pronounced like ' *pick't her.*'

This type of pronunciation has long been abolished in polite English, but the above spellings show that the following rhymes of **Swift** are based on the old usage: *hectors–lectures*; *stricter–picture, venture–enter*. The last rhyme occurs also in **Gray**.

CHAPTER III
VOWEL QUANTITY

Rhymes Based upon Vowel Quantity Different from that of To-day.

THIS class of rhyme is very disconcerting to the reader of the early poets who is ill-equipped with a knowledge of English philology, and these rhymes are probably among the first to be set down by him as ' bad ' and ' careless.'

The first thing to realise in judging such rhymes is that there are a fairly large number of words which had long vowels in M.E., notably in Chaucer, in which the vowel has been shortened since his time. The Elizabethans and their successors still preserved the old long vowels in many words in which we have shortened them. This shortening process has not been consistently carried out in present-day Standard English. Thus, while we have a short vowel in *breath, dread, wet*, we retain the length in *weed, to read, seat*; we have shortening in *fret, get, stead*, but have the old quantity in *meat, seat, bead*; we shorten in *sweat*, and *shed* (verb), but not in *heat* and *lead* (verb); in *dead, death, head, deaf, red* (colour), but not in *leaf, beat, leap, great*. Here we have four originally distinct groups of words from the point of view of O.E., but in M.E. they formed one large group and all had the same *long* vowel—$\bar{e}^2$ ($\hat{e}$).

86

The fact that some of these words are still spelt with *ea* points to the probability that they were commonly pronounced with a long vowel, at any rate as late as the time when the spelling was fixed —that is, so far as this group is concerned, during the latter part of the sixteenth or the first quarter of the seventeenth century.   The symbol *ea* was not generally used to express a short vowel.

On the other hand, the shortening process had certainly begun in the age of Shakespeare, as both some rhymes and Occasional Spellings testify. It would appear as though, while the old long type was more usual, the shortened types were also used by some speakers, and both types were known to the poets.   Indeed, they sometimes appear to use shortened forms of words in which we have kept the long vowel—*e.g.*, Shakespeare's *steps-leaps* (' Venus and Adonis,' l. 279) (*cf.* p. 90).

Cowley, who, by the way, is almost the last poet in whom I have noted the survival of the long vowel in words where we have shortened it, uses both the long form of *sweat*, rhyming with *seat*, and the short, rhyming with *set*.   Apparently, after the first half of the seventeenth century the forms with shortened vowels became more and more universal.

It is sometimes possible to account for a shortened vowel by a well-known phonetic principle which produces shortening before certain combinations of consonants.   Thus, if we have reason to assume a shortened pronunciation of the vowel in *great*, as when Milton rhymes it with *set* (' Ode on the Nativity, ll. 120-121), this form may be transferred from the Comparative *gretter*, a common form and spelling in the sixteenth century, from M.E. *grĕtre*, where the originally long vowel (O.E. *grēatra*) was shortened in M.E. before *-tr-* (cp. *gretter*, p. 100). On the other hand, the vowel in *great* itself may have been shortened as that in *leap* was shortened, or as we have shortened that in *head* or *wet*, etc.

For the convenience of those whose knowledge of M.E. quantities is not as good as, let us hope, it once was, we give an alphabetical list of words which had a long *ē*² in M.E. though they now have a short vowel. In the list of rhymes which follows it will be seen that most of these words occur rhymed with words in which the long vowel is preserved at the present day. It is a reasonable inference that the poets intended both or all the words of this type which they thus put together to be pronounced with long vowels, and that they were justified in this because their contemporaries still adhered to the old quantity in these words.

If the rhymes of this class which are unsatisfactory according to present-day usage can be shown to have been perfectly good rhymes, at least down to the seventeenth century, a large element of what is often too hastily regarded as carelessness in the earlier poets is at once removed.

Words which in M.E. had a Long Vowel, ē², now Shortened.

The following all had long vowels in the language of Chaucer:

Bread, breath, dead, deaf, death, dread (noun and verb), *forget* (M.E. *-yēte*), *fret*, 'devour,' *get* (M.E. *yēte*), *head, heaven, heavy* (long type in Shakespeare's rhyme *heavy–leafy* and in *havey*, a seventeenth-century form cited p. 90), *let*, *never* (M.E. *nĕvre*, and *nēver*), *red* (the colour), *ready* (M.E. *rĕdye*, *rĕdie*, when inflected), *shed* (verb, M.E. *shēde*, infinitive and present; preterite *shĕdde*, *shădde*), *spread* (M.E. *sprēde*, infinitive and present; preterite *sprĕdde*, *sprădde*), *stead* (noun), ' place,' *sweat* (noun and verb), *thread* (noun and verb), *threat* (noun and verb), *tred* (verb), *wet* (noun and verb).

Rhymes in which One of the Words now has a Short Vowel while the Other Preserves the Older Length of Vowel.

Udall's ' Roister Doister,' *alreadie–greedy*, *threaten–beaten*. **Wyatt,** *eaten–threaten*; *freat* (fret)–*great*; *heate–freate*; *dreade–leade* (verb); *sweate* (verb)–*heate*; *drede–spede–dede* (*speed*, has *ē*[1]). **Surrey,** *drede–dede*. **Sackville,** *dread–need*. **Spenser,** *get her–greater* (see remarks on *gretter*, p. 100; it is quite possible that Spenser intends long vowels in both cases); *breath–beneath–death*; *intreat–heat–sweat*; *heate–threat–beate–seate*; *greate – sweate*. **Shakespeare,** *entreats – frets*; *heat – get*; *sweat – heat*; *heaven – even*; *dread – mead*; *sheds – bleeds – proceeds*; *pleadeth – dreadeth – leadeth*; *heavy–leafy*. **Drayton,** *wreath–breath*; *lead* (verb)–*tread*; *breath – heath*. **Donne,** *eate – meate – sweate*; *breath – underneath*; *great – get*. **Habington,** *lead* (verb)–*tread–dead*; *beneath–bequeath–breath*. **Milton,** *spreads–meads*; *great–set*; *eat–wet* ('Penseroso,' l. 80); *wet–great* (' Penseroso,' l. 8). **Cowley,** *intreat–threat*; *heat–beget*; *heat–sweat*. **Dryden,** *bread–feed*. (If this is a genuine rhyme it implies that Dryden still pronounced *bread* long, and with ' *ea* ' according to new type, since *feed* has $\bar{e}^1$, and had long been pronounced as at present; *cf.* p. 61.) **Pope** rhymes *dead–shade*, with M.E. length in former word.

It has been said that all the words in the above list had long vowels in Chaucer's time. In many of them we still pronounce long vowels. It is reasonable to suppose that in the sixteenth and seventeenth centuries a larger number than at present still preserved the old quantity. The evidence of this, apart from the rhymes, is not so copious as could be wished. Of Occasional Spellings which point to a long vowel where we have a short, I have noted *beheedyd*, ' beheaded,' in Lord Berners' *Froissart*; *preaty* in Latimer's sermons; *threed*, ' thread,' in Lily's *Euphues*; Lady Hobart, Verney Memoirs (1679), writes *havey* for ' heavy,' and this apparently is identical with Shakespeare's type rhyming with *leafy* (p. 89). This lady would probably have written her (and Shakespeare's) pronunciation of *leafy*, ' *lavey*.'

From the seventeenth-century Grammarians we may note that Wharton (1654) gives *bread* and *bred* as respectively long and short; that Cooper (1685) includes *sweat* (verb) in the same list as *seat* among words nearly all of which contain a long vowel down to the present time; that Baker (1725) says that the vowels in *deaf, breath, sweat,* and *threat* are all long.

To sum up, the old vowel $\bar{e}^2$ appears to have been shortened among certain sections of the community during the sixteenth century under conditions which it is difficult to formulate precisely, but especially before *d, t, th* (voiceless as in *breath*). The shortened forms passed gradually into Standard English, and are occasionally used by the poets, who, however,

at any rate down to Dryden, appear to have preferred the old long forms which were still current
in Standard English. At the present time we use a
larger proportion of forms with a shortened vowel
than was usual in Dryden's time. The fact, however,
that we still retain a large number of words in which
the vowel is not shortened shows that Standard
English in this as in many other respects is a blend
of several dialect types.

Now for the other side of the picture. It has been
mentioned that the old poets, to judge by their
rhymes, do use, occasionally, the shortened type.
We shall see that they even use as rhymes with
words which were undoubtedly short in their day,
as in ours, words in which the vowel had always
been short; others in which it was long in M.E.,
and in which present-day Standard English retains
the old long vowel. The old poets, in fact, sometimes go further than we do in the direction of
shortening. It looks very much as though all the
$\bar{e}^2$ words existed, as they perhaps still exist, in living
popular dialects, in the shortened form, just as
probably other dialects still keep the unshortened
forms of all of them, not necessarily all in the same
dialect, but here or there throughout the country.
It seems to be a pure accident that Standard English
has at last settled down quite definitely to the use
of the long type in some words and the shortened
type in others.

The list from the poets is not a large one as
regards this particular vowel, but we shall see that
the evidence of the Occasional Spellings and the
Grammarians confirms the early existence of the
shortened forms.

the shortening of the vowel occurred in M.E. before the double consonants *-dde, -tte*, as in *lēden* (infinitive), *lĕdde* (preterite), *mēten–mĕtte*, etc.

There are several spellings which imply shortening of *ē²* before *-t, -st*, etc.   Sir Thomas Elyot writes *hedde*, ' head,' in his *Gouernour* (1531); Lord Berners (translation of Froissart, 1529) has *presst*, ' priest '; Machyn has *mett*, ' meat,' *swett*, ' sweat,' *heddes*, ' heads ' (1550); Cavendish (*Life of Wolsey*, 1577) has *strett*, ' street '; Lily (*Euphues*), *beheaddest*.

It seems that the short types of the words we have been considering were in use from the first quarter of the sixteenth century at any rate; that the words with a shortened vowel do not altogether coincide with those of the same type now in use in Standard English; that the actual distribution of the two types in Standard English was probably fixed by the middle of the eighteenth century.

Shortening of Other Vowels, especially before Voiceless Consonants.

The provincial dialects at the present day often have short vowels in words where we have long ones. Standard English itself has unaccountably shortened vowels in some words, yet preserved the original length of precisely the same vowels in other words. Thus we have a short vowel in *hot*, from M.E. *hōte*— a word not infrequently written *hoate* in the sixteenth century—which points to a still surviving long vowel.   Yet we have kept the old long in *wrote, throat, boat*, and many more.   It need not surprise us to find that in this as in many other respects the habits of our ancestors, though perhaps no less inconsistent, did not exactly correspond to our own.

We have had to deal specially with the difficult words of the *flood* type, the vowel of which represents a very important shortening process (pp. 75–82), but a few examples may be given of some sixteenth-century shortenings revealed by Occasional Spellings which are foreign to present-day Standard English so far as the particular words are concerned.

Lord Berners in his translation of Froissart has *loffe*, ' loaf,' *roffes*, ' roofs,' *bottes*, ' boats,' *rodde*, ' rode '; Cavendish has *botts*, ' boats '; *smot*, ' smote,' occurs in the First Folio of Shakespeare. Wharton writes *yuth*, *yung* for ' youth,' ' young,' which, he says, have the same vowel as ' *dubble*.' Butler says the vowel of *reek*, ' rick,' is short.

One would be inclined to dismiss Shakespeare's rhyme of *teeth–with* as ' mere carelessness,' but for the shortenings noted above before *-f* in Lord Berners, Wharton's shortening before *-th*, and, above all, for the definite statement of Baker, as late as 1724, that the vowels in *tooth* and *teeth* are short.

Certainly there is a vulgar pronunciation to-day of *tooth* and *roof* with a short vowel. Drayton has a curious rhyme, *beech* (the tree) with *wych*, but the vowel in the first word may have been shortened before *-ch*, as it is in the word *breeches*, in spite of the spelling, and that of *reach* apparently is when Drayton rhymes it with *stretch*. *Reach* may be heard with a short vowel to-day in the provincial dialects.

Long and Short Vowels before -s, -st, -f, -ft, -th, etc.

There are certain difficulties connected with the quantity of English vowels before the above consonants which cannot be cleared up without further very careful investigation. There appear to have been at least two periods during which there was a tendency to lengthen short vowels when followed by -s, -st, etc., and it is also probable that at an early period long vowels were shortened in this position.

O.E. *gāst* becomes M.E. *gōst*, ' ghost, spirit,' and shows apparently the normal change of O.E. long *ā* to *ō*, but it is by no means certain that in the nominative case the regular process was not that the vowel of O.E. *gāst* underwent a shortening before becoming *ō*, giving *gǎst* in the nominative singular. If this is so, then M.E. *gōst* must be explained from the analogy of the inflected cases —*gāstes*, etc.—where the syllable division was *gā-stes*, which normally became *gōstes* because the two consonants which, occurring in the nominative at the close of the syllable, produced shortening of the preceding vowel, in the inflected cases, instead of closing the first syllable, begin the next. The shortening is seen in M.E. *fǐst*, O.E. *fȳst, fīst*. In the former case the type of the inflected cases has become generalised, in the latter that of the uninflected nominative singular. The survival of long vowels in many words before -st must be explained in the same way as that of the long vowel in *ghost*. The question is complicated by the fact that at a later date than this shortening before -st, some time during the fifteenth century, short vowels appear to have undergone lengthening before -*st*, etc., and also before -*s*, and -*ft*. The result of this process is heard in the vowel in *host, post, toast, coast, roast* as we now pronounce these words.

This is not all; there is another group of words such as *cost, toss, froth, soft* which, in the pronunciation of many people, have also a long vowel, though of an entirely different quality from that in *toast, coast*, etc. It will be noted, further, that an equal number of good speakers pronounce a short vowel in *cost, froth*, etc. The lengthening of the vowel in words of this class is probably quite recent, having taken place perhaps within the last century or so. It is hard to say whether the lengthened type in *cost*, etc., is gaining ground in Standard English or not.

Such a rhyme as *lost–boast*, which we find in Shakespeare, according to present-day standards might pass as an assonance, but is no rhyme at all, since the lengthened type of *lost* has now a totally different vowel from that in *boast*. The etymology of *boast* is very doubtful, and we do not know whether the vowel was originally long, or lengthened by the fifteenth-century process, but the sound would be the same in either case. On the other hand, the vowel in *toast* is certainly due to this later lengthening, and we must suppose that if that in *lost* had undergone this process the result would have been the same, and the word would have been a perfect rhyme with *boast*. I have unfortunately no collateral evidence of the existence of a lengthened type in *lost* itself, but Hodges (1643) gives the pairs *toss'd–toast, cost–coast, bost (i.e.,* furnished with bosses)–

boast, as being pronounced ' near alike.' Cooper says that *o* is nearly always long before -*st*, and gives *frost* as an example.

Further, there are a few Occasional Spellings which distinctly point to a lengthening of vowels before -*s*, -*st*, -*ft*, and -*th*—namely, *toossed* in Bishop Latimer's sermons; *geest*, ' guest ' (Coventry Leet Book, 1443); *Roister Doister*, l. 1, *gueast* rhymes with *feast*; and *crooft*, ' small farm, croft ' (Coventry Leet Book, 1422, 1423); *moathes*, ' moths,' in Lily's *Euphues*; and in a seventeenth-century letter of Lady Verney. It might certainly be assumed that the long vowels here implied are the ancestors of those often heard at the present day in *toss, croft,* etc., and I formerly took that view. On the other hand, we can only account for the vowel in *toast* on the one hand and that in the present-day long type of *tossed* on the other, by assuming two processes of lengthening—an earlier which produced the former word, and a later which produced the second form. Further, if the long vowels suggested by the spellings in Coventry Leet Book and Bishop Latimer were really the actual predecessors of the ' *aw* ' sound now heard in *toss* and *croft*, we must disbelieve Hodges when he tells us that in his day *toss'd* and *toast* were ' near alike '—identical would perhaps have been his word but for the difference of spelling—although, if he is right, this justifies rhymes used by Shakespeare and later poets.

I have noted the following rhymes of words now containing ' long *o*,' often spelt *oa*, with others which now have either ' short *o* ' or the later lengthening of this; and of ' long *ea* ' with ' short *e* ':

Spenser, *boast–most–tost* (past participle). **Shake-speare,** *guest–feast* (*cf. geest* above); *jest–beast*; *lost–boast.* **Drayton,** *lost – coast, –boast, cross'd – host.* **Milton,** *feast–guest–least; feast–rest–request.* **Cowley,** *least–rest; best–least; east–best.* **Dryden,** *boast–lost; feast–guest; lost–coast; coast–toss'd.* **Waller,** *lost–coast; feasts–guests; guest–priest.* **Pope,** *guests–beasts.*

Owing to the imperfection of our knowledge, pending a thorough investigation of the whole problem of lengthenings and shortenings in English, it is impossible to say whether in such rhymes as *guest–priest* we ought to assume that the first word had its vowel lengthened as suggested by the spelling *geest* above quoted, or that the second word had its vowel shortened as suggested by the spelling *presst* quoted p. 93.

The question is very obscure, and is not made easier by remarkable diversity of habit as regards quantity existing in English dialects, and in different periods of the language, a diversity which is reflected in the rhymes of the poets, in the statements of the Grammarians, and the evidence afforded by the Occasional Spellings.

The net result of the foregoing discussion seems to be that the poets, on the whole, employed only such forms, whether long or short, as were in actual use—that is, that their rhymes were real rhymes based on pronunciations current in their day.

The reader must not expect to find in this, or in any other part of this little book, direct evidence on the contemporary pronunciation of every indi-vidual word made use of by the poets in rhyme. If it can be established that *cost* could be pronounced

like *coast* and *toss'd* like *toast*, then it is a legitimate
influence that *lost* could be, and was, pronounced
so as to form a perfect rhyme with *boast*. Again,
if two pronunciations of a word were current, such
as '*geest*' and '*guěst*,' the same poet might use both
as occasion demanded, especially at a time when the
standard was not nearly so definitely fixed as at
present.

Words which have now Short Vowels, Rhymed by Early Poets with Others having Long Vowels.
Variations in Quantity of Vowels due to Inflexion.

Many words in M.E. had normally a short vowel
in the nominative singular, but a long vowel in all
inflected cases. Thus *blăk*, ' black,' but *blāke* when
a noun followed and the adjective took the inflec-
tional suffix -*e*; *Gŏd*, but *Gōdes* (genitive singular),
Gōde (dative), and so on. This is due to the fact
that in M.E. a short vowel was lengthened in ' open '
syllables—that is, syllables which did not end in
a consonant. The syllable division in the genitive
and dative was *Gō-des*, *Gō-de*, etc.; in the nominative singular the syllable ' closed' by the consonant
d, and no lengthening took place. As a rule the one
type or the other appears to have been used after a
time for all cases, so that a speaker either said
Gōd, *blāk*, etc., in the uninflected nominative singular on the analogy of the inflected forms with a long
vowel, or *Gŏdes*, *blăke* in the inflected forms, on the
model of the unlengthened type. In some words
in present-day English we use the lengthened type;
thus *bead*, *yoke*, *tame* are from the inflected types
bēde, *yōke*, *tāme*, of which the old uninflected nomina-

tives were *bĕd, yŏk, tăm*; while *back, glad, sad* are from the old unlengthened uninflected types. In *cot* we have the descendant of the old nominative singular; in *cote* that of the dative, etc. It is certain that many words survived far beyond the M.E. period in both types, and this double usage is reflected in the rhymes of the early poets, and sometimes in Occasional Spellings—*e.g.*, Sir Thomas Elyot's *yocke* is evidently from the old uninflected type.

Allusion has been made (pp. 87, 88) to the shortening of some adjectives in the comparative as in M.E. *grĕttre, dĕppre*, also *grĕtter, dĕpper* from earlier *grētra, dēopra*. *Grĕtter*, etc., survives far into the fifteenth century in this spelling in prose, just as the pronunciation does much later in the rhymes (*cf.* Spenser's *get her–greater*, p. 89).* It is possible that the shortened *grĕt* (so spelt) in ' Rede me and be not wroth ' (seen also in Milton's rhyme, *great–set*, p. 92) may have been formed on the analogy of the comparative, though the vowel here may have been independently shortened before -*t* (*cf.* p. 88).

Rhymes Implying Type Derived from Inflected Form, where we now Use that Derived from Uninflected Form.

Black.—Sackville rhymes this with *lake*, indicating survival of M.E. *blāke*; this type now survives only in the family name *Blake*. *Cf.* Chaucer's rhyme with this type:

> *For fēre of blāke bēres or bōles blāke*
> *Or elles blāke develes wole hem tāke.—*
>
> NONNE PREESTES TALE, 115-16.

---

* The spellings *depper* ' deeper,' *swetter* 'sweeter,' fr. *swētra*, also occur in the fifteenth century.

Small.—Surrey rhymes this word (spelt *smale*) with *tale–pale–scale–bale*. The rhyme here is perfect as the type *smale* is the M.E. inflected form *smāle*, as in Chaucer's *And smāle foules māken melodīe*, which now survives only in the family name *Smale*. Our *small* is from the nominative O.E. *smæl*, M.E. *smǎl*. Exactly parallel with the development of the *smale* type is that of *whale*, M.E. *whāle*, from inflected type; but Nom. *whǎl*, O.E. *hwæl*.

God.—Rhymed by **Milton** with *abode* and *untrod*, further with *load* and *rod*; by **Dryden** with *abode*; by **Pope** with *road*; by **Gray** with *abode*.

This survival of the M.E. type *Gōd*, from the inflected forms, is vouched for by Price (1668), who says that *God* and *goad* are pronounced alike. The above rhymes may therefore be accepted as perfect. Another type with a long vowel, which may be popularly expressed by the spelling *gawd*, is due to a late lengthening of the old short type, comparable to, though not necessarily contemporary with, that in *cost, froth*, etc. (*cf.* pp. 96, 97). This type, now a vulgarism, is clearly indicated by Otway's spelling *Gaud*, and in Pope's rhyme of this word with *unawed* ('Dunciad,' iii., ll. 223-224).

Grass.—Rhymed by **Sackville** with *place* and *space*. This might be explained from M.E. *grāse*, etc., compared with nominative *grǎs*, whence our present form is derived. We should expect the *s* in the M.E. inflected forms to become *z* between vowels (*cf. graze*, verb, and *glaze*, verb from *glass*). The vowel assumed in Sackville's rhyme is identical with that in these two verbs, the *s* could be explained by an analogy with the Nominative type.

Survival of Long Vowel before -nd.

The word *friend*, M.E. *frēnd, freend*, O.E. *frēond*, had a long vowel long after the M.E. period. Our type with shortened vowel is usually explained as due to the analogy of the compound *friendship*, M.E. *frĕndschippe*, in which the vowel was normally shortened before the combination of consonants *-ndsch-*. The word *fiend*, which still retains the original long vowel of M.E. *feend*, O.E. *fēond*. In the word *end* the vowel, though originally short, was lengthened in late O.E. before *-nd*, which normally preserves the quantity of old long vowels, and lengthens earlier short ones. Thus in M.E. we get the spelling *eend*. It is rather difficult to account for the short vowel in the present-day form. Both this word and *friend* occur in the old poets, rhyming with words whose vowels were undoubtedly long.

The doggrel tract, ' *Rede me and be not wroth* ' (1529), has *endes–fendes*, ' fiends '; Shakespeare, *fiendes–friends*; Milton rhymes *end* with *fiend*.

Butler (1641) says that *friend* has the sound of *ee*; Wallis (1654) gives *friend* as having the same vowel as *fiend*; Wharton (1654) writes *freend*. Cooper (1685) writes *eend* to express the pronunciation of *end*.

Old Long Vowels Preserved, and Old Short Vowels Lengthened before -ld.

The vowel in O.E. *hēold*, ' held,' preserves its length in M.E. *heeld*. This type survives in Spenser's rhyme *beheld–seeld* (' seldom,' M.E. *sēld*), and in

Milton's *shield–withheld*. The vowel in *shield* was long in M.E. as now, being lengthened in late O.E. from earlier *scĕld*, before *-ld*. It should be mentioned that Milton also rhymes *held–repelled–spelled* where the first word has apparently a short vowel as at present.

In **Waller's** rhymes *build–field*, *builds–shields*, and in **Dryden's** *yields–fields–builds*, the last word, though spelt as at present, probably represents quite a different dialect type, the South-Eastern or 'Kentish' M.E. *bēlde(n)*. This type occurs in the Oseney Register, *beeldid*, and in Machyn (1550) *beldyd*. Just as M.E. *schĕld* has produced *shield*, and *fĕld*, *field*, so M.E. *hĕld* had it survived would probably have been spelt **hield*, and M.E. *bēlde* would have been spelt **bield*, and the words would have all been perfect rhymes with each other, as they were in M.E. and in the sixteenth and seventeenth centuries. There is nothing surprising in the use of a South-Easternism such as *beeld*, by Waller and Dryden, since this very form was in use in the preceding century by the Cockney Machyn, and many other words of this dialect type were in use in the sixteenth and seventeenth centuries which have now been replaced by an East Midland type, as in *build*. Nor is it incredible that a form should be disguised to the eye by a spelling belonging to a different type—to this day we *pronounce* a South-Eastern type in *bury* (='berry'), though we spell it according to a Westerly type. Rhyme not infrequently reveals the writer's pronunciation though the conventional spelling may disguise it.

Variants Produced by Differences of Stress or Emphasis.

Long treatises might be—indeed, have been—written on the influence of stress on English vowel sounds. The vowels in the unstressed syllables of words develop quite differently from the same original vowels in fully stressed syllables.

There are also certain independent words which may occur sometimes in a stressed position in the sentence, sometimes in an unstressed, and which are pronounced differently according to the degree of emphasis which they receive. The chief classes of such words are personal pronouns, prepositions, and auxiliary verbs.

These differences occur regularly in natural speech at the present day, and they occurred also in the older periods of the language. It may happen that the descendant of a weak (*i.e.*, unstressed) form which arose in M.E. becomes later on the only one current, the other type, that occurring in the stressed position, falling out of use. Some of the apparent imperfections of the rhymes of the older poets are due to the fact that they are using an old variant of a word which we have lost. The ordinary reader cannot penetrate the veil of the spelling.

The present *are, have, shall* are old unstressed forms, the descendants of the M.E. stressed types being no longer used. On the other hand, in *do, to* we have preserved the old strong, stressed forms, but have lost the other unstressed types of these words. We certainly have, at the present day, both stressed and unstressed forms of all these words, but in *are, have, shall* we use the descendants of the old weak forms, in stressed positions, and have formed new weak forms, from these which we use in unstressed positions. In *do, to* our present weak forms are not the descendants of the old unstressed forms but new formations.

Are.—In M.E. the stressed form was *āre(n)*, the unstressed *ăr(e)*. The descendant of the former, however we chose to spell it, would, had it survived, have been pronounced exactly like the word *air*, and would thus have rhymed perfectly with *care*, etc.

That this type was in use late into the seventeenth century at any rate is proved by the statement of Price that *are* and *air* are alike in sound, and that of Cooper that *are, air, heir, ere* all sound alike. In the Verney Memoirs *are* is spelt *air, aier*. We find *air* written by comic writers of the nineteenth century—*e.g.*, Dickens, though only as representing the speech of vulgar persons.

The very different form which alone survives in polite speech as the emphatic type of this auxiliary is derived from the M.E. unstressed type *ăr*, which, when used in stressed positions, is lengthened, besides having undergone other changes in its vowel sound into which we need not now enter.

The following brief list of rhymes would seem to show that the descendant of the M.E. *āre* form was in use among good speakers at any rate to near the middle of the eighteenth century.

Rede me and be not wroth, *are–weare* (of clothes). Spenser, *are–compare*. Shakespeare, *unaware–are, –snare; compare–are*. Donne, *are–faire, –declare*.

Habington, *are–prayer, –care, –were, –faire.* Milton, *pair–are.* Suckling, *are–aware.* Waller, *are–spare.* Cowley, *are–despair, –declare, –hear, –there, –fair.* Swift, *are–care–bear.* Pope, *are–care.*

Have.—Since the stressed form in M.E. was *hăve*, we naturally find this in Chaucer rhyming with *grāve*, and so on.

It is probable that many poets at the present time would not hesitate to use such rhymes for this word, and this is due to the similarity in spelling whereby they appeal to the eye, and partly, perhaps, to tradition also. But such a tradition would never have arisen had the rhymes not once been good, as we should hardly expect a conspiracy of poets to make a bad rhyme traditional by repeated use. We find the old strong type still surviving in the compound *behave.*

The following are a few of the words which the various poets rhyme with *have*:

Sackville, *grave, wave*; Spenser, *save, gave, grave*; Shakespeare, *have it–grave it, slave*; Drayton, *brave*; Donne, *grave*; Milton, *save, gave*; Suckling, *crave*; Waller, *grave*; Cowley and Dryden, *crave*; Pope, *wave*, etc.

Shall.—The M.E. *ă* in the combination *-al-* in stressed syllables, when final as in *all, small*, etc., or when followed by another consonant, as in *salt, halt*, etc., is first diphthongised to *au*, and this develops early into the present ' *aw* ' sound. The old stressed form of *shall* therefore would, did it survive in Standard English, undoubtedly be pronounced exactly like the word *shawl*. Our present form may be explained in two ways: it may represent an old unstressed form, or it may have originated in such combination as *shall I*, etc. Neither in an unstressed position in the sentence, nor when followed by a vowel as in *shall I*, would the vowel of the word have undergone diphthongisation and the subsequent vowel change. There is, therefore, no difficulty in explaining the present-day pronunciation of *shall*.

A few examples have been noted of the other type in the sixteenth century:

Udall (*Roister Doister*) rhymes *shall–all*; Spenser, *shall–gall, –thrall, –all*.

The spelling *schawl* occurs in the late fifteenth-century Cely Papers. The seventeenth-century Grammarians Wharton and Cooper both include *shall* in their lists of ' *awe* ' words, together with *all, ball*, etc.

The present writer has heard ' *shawl* ' for *shall* a few years ago from a young Cambridge man whose home was in the North of Ireland, in stressed position at the end of a sentence—Y*es, I shawl*, and so on.

Do.—The present-day pronunciation of this word is normally derived from the stressed M.E. *dōn*, but in the stereotyped combination *don't* we have an entirely different development. This must represent a M.E. shortened form, and the combination must have been stressed *dŏnót*. In this short form the vowel *ŏ* arose before the long *o* developed to its present *oo* (*ū*) sound. In *don't* the stress must have been shifted later on to the first word, whose vowel then underwent lengthening, while the second word which was not unstressed lost its vowel altogether. The independent word *do* occurs in

Pope, rhyming with *show.*   This type, again a lengthened form of the old M.E. unstressed and shortened
form which must have arisen in the auxiliary use
of the word, is vouched for by Cooper, who says that
do is pronounced like *doe* (the animal).   But for this
entry of Cooper's I should have been inclined at first
to set down Pope's rhyme as a bad one, but in the
face of this statement, and when we remember *don't,*
whose vowel can only be accounted for in the
manner suggested above, one is inclined to accept
Pope's rhyme as a good, though I think rare, one,
and to explain the development as a survival of the
weak auxiliary.

To.—Cooper says that this word is pronounced like
the noun *tow.*   Such a pronunciation of the preposition can only be derived from M.E. unstressed,
and shortened *tŏ* which was later adopted as a strong
form, and lengthened after the strong *tō* had already
assumed its present form.   The earlier M.E. weak
form of the word is written *te* in many early texts.

CHAPTER IV

CONSONANTS

Rhymes Based on a Pronunciation of Consonants Different from that of the Present Day.

PERHAPS there is no more striking difference between the English of refined and educated persons in the sixteenth, seventeenth, and early eighteenth centuries and in our own day than the pronunciation of certain consonants. Many of these pronunciations can be traced, from the Occasional Spellings, as far back as the fifteenth century, some of them further back still. They are of various kinds: the substitution of one consonant for another; assimilations of consonants occurring in groups; the complete loss of consonantal sounds, especially when final; the addition of a consonant at the end of a word. There is no doubt that some of these processes, if exhibited at the present day, would produce an impression of extreme vulgarity and illiteracy. Yet during the two centuries preceding the death of Pope the frequent spellings which occur in private documents, written by highly educated persons, and even in published works, leave no doubt that the features referred to must have been commonly current in the ordinary speech of the upper classes, no less than in that of some below these. The earliest Grammarians hardly refer to these things—possibly because they were too much part and parcel of everyday usage to call for comment; possibly, in some cases, because they simply declined to recognise such violent departures from the supposedly ' correct ' forms recorded by the orthodox spelling. The Grammarians of the later seventeenth century face facts more frankly and record a certain number of these pronunciations, though not always with approval, designating them as ' barbarous,' and so on; but Jones, at the beginning of the eighteenth century, describes still more, as though they were the ordinary rule, and without comment. Towards the end of the century the Scotchman Elphinstone, only too eager to find fault with the way the English spoke their own language, describes many of these vagaries, generally saying that they belong to the vulgar speech of London. Probably by the end of his life —he died in 1809—these pronunciations were falling into disrepute, and survived chiefly among the old in the upper classes, or in a much lower stratum of society.

I have noted a certain number of rhymes which are evidently based upon consonantal pronunciations quite alien to polite speech at the present time, but perfectly in keeping with it at the time the poems were written. The pronunciation which the poet has in mind is usually concealed beneath the approved spelling, which, indeed, shows that he considered it as natural and that his readers would automatically supply the required pronunciation.

Substitution of One Consonant for Another.

1. **-f for -th.**—Instances of this are very fairly common in the Occasional Spellings in the sixteenth and down to the middle of the seventeenth century. Examples of these have been already given in the Introduction, p. 23 above. To these may be added the remarkable form *helfe* for *health* which occurs in the Alleyne Papers (1593), pp. 15 and 16. This corresponds exactly with Wyatt's rhyme *helth–self*, which we might have been inclined to dismiss as a mere assonance but for John Alleyne. Hodges sets down *death* and *deaf* as ' near alike,' which no doubt means that he pronounced *f* in the former word.

2. **-f for -gh.**—Many words in present-day Standard English show a change of the sound formerly expressed by *gh* to *f*, although the old spelling is usually retained—*e.g.*, *laugh*, *laughter*, *enough*, etc. In others the old sound of *gh* has simply disappeared, as in *through*, *taught*, *daughter*, etc. In the sixteenth and seventeenth centuries, however, the type with *f* was used in many of these in polite speech. Margaret Paston writes *throf*, ' through ' (1465); the Verneys and their friends and relations frequently write *dafter*; Hodges says that *ought* and *oft* are pronounced ' near alike '; Butler writes *dafter*, ' daughter '; Jones (1701) says that *f* is pronounced in *bought*, *taught*, and *nought*.

Surrey rhymes *tought*, ' taught,' and *aloft* (*Tottel*, p. 23); and **Marston** rhymes *after–dafter* (*Eastward Hoe*, v. 1, 1604); **Roister Doister** rhymes *manslaughter–laughter*, and as *laugh* is several times

written with *f* about this time it is probable that
'*slafter–lafter*' is intended. Baker (1725) says
slaughter is pronounced *slafter*.

3. **Final -s, or -ce, becomes -sh.**—Only one example
of this has been noted in the rhymes—*prince–ynch*
in '*Rede me and be not wroth*'—which may seem
hardly worth mentioning. But *-sh* for *-s* is pretty
frequent in the spellings from the fifteenth century
onwards, and the very form in the above rhyme
actually occurs in Machyn (1550)—*the prynche of
Spaine*, pp. 51 and 52. Besides this, *blesshing* is
found (1460) in the Oseney Register; *a powter
vesshell* (Margaret Paston, 1461); *kysshed* in Caxton's
Jason, p. 85, l. 35; *hushband* in Basire Correspondence; *winch'd* in Congreve's *Old Bachelor*. Elphinstone notes with disapproval *cutlash*, etc., and
also *Poarchmouth*, which, strange to say, in the form
Porchmouth is found at least thrice in a letter of
Sir Henry Seymour (1544), and by three separate
letter-writers in the Verney Memoirs between 1665
and 1680. There can be no doubt of the genuine-
ness of these pronunciations, nor of that suggested
by the above rhyme.

4. **Final -ing becomes -in.**—Rhymes like *viewing–
ruin* may be found in most poets from Shakespeare
to Wordsworth and Tennyson. It is unnecessary
to collect examples. The rhymes of this class were
perfect, and it is quite certain that down to the
thirties of the last century *-in* and not *-ing* was the
almost universal pronunciation among all classes
of speakers—in fact, many thousands of excellent
speakers never use any other form to-day. The
spellings in *-yn, -in* from the fourteenth century on-

wards are very numerous. In the sixteenth century such writers as Sir Richard Gresham and Queen Elizabeth may be mentioned who have spellings of this kind; they are very abundant in the Verney Memoirs and in the Wentworth Papers. Swift (*Polite Conversations*) includes *learnen* among the pronunciations used ' by the chief patterns of politeness at Court, at Levees,' etc. Swift appears to deride such a pronunciation, though his poems teem with rhymes like *garden–farthing* (then called ' *fardin* '), *linen–grinning*, *picking–chicken*, and so on. Even the fastidious Cooper says that *coughing* and *coffin*, *cummin* and *coming* are pronounced alike.

Rhymes Implying Loss of Consonants.

1. **Loss of r before -s and -ch.**—We have now lost the sound of *r* everywhere in Standard English before consonants, but we have lengthened the preceding vowel to make up for this. Thus the vowel in *burst* was originally short, but was gradually lengthened as the sound of *r* was weakened. The rhymes to be mentioned are based, however, on a much earlier loss of *r* which took place in the fifteenth century at latest before -s and -*ch*, and which was not accompanied by lengthening of the preceding vowel. Some of these old forms survive as vulgarisms or as jocular colloquialisms such as ' *cuss* ' for *curse*, and ' *bust* ' for *burst*. These pronunciations have a most respectable antiquity and were formerly in polite use. The oldest rhyme noted is much older than the *r*-less spellings, but there is no doubt that it is genuine—Bokenam in ' Lives of the Saints ' (1443) rhymes *adust*, ' in the dust ' with

wurst, ' worst.' Machyn writes *Wosseter* and *Dasset*; *fust,* ' first,' occurs in Verney Memoirs (1642); Cooper (1685) gives *wusted* (as at present) for *worsted*; and Baker (1724) says that *thirsty, nurse, Ursula,* etc., are pronounced as *thusty, nus, Usly,* etc. The soundness of the following rhymes is therefore perfectly established.

Roister Doister, *cust,* ' *curs'd* '–*must*; Rede me and be not wroth, *such–church*; Surrey, *furst–dust* (*cf. fust* in Verney Memoirs); Dryden, *burst–dust,* with which we may compare the colloquial ' *bust.*'

2. Loss of -l before -n.—The sound of *l* is normally lost at the present time before *k, f, m, b* (*cf. walk, calf, calm,* etc.). Except in the river name *Colne* and place name *Calne* it is not lost in stressed syllables before *-n.* (For the case of *l* before *d* in unstressed syllables see remarks on *would, should,* etc., p. 129, etc., below.) In *realm* the sound has now been ' restored ' (see this word, p. 128 below).

Surrey has what looks like a preposterous rhyme at first sight — *bemoan – swolne* (' swollen '); and Drayton rhymes *swoln* with *Colne,* which, presumably, was pronounced as now, without *l.* Surrey's rhyme is, however, proved to be in accordance with the pronunciation of his day by his contemporary Machyn's spelling, *swone.*

3. Loss of final t after k sound, and after k before s.—The following would be considered slovenly rhymes at the present time:

Habington, *countercheck–direct*; Captain Ratcliff (in Dryden's ' Miscellany '), *project–logick*; Swift, *directs–circumflex*; Pope, *sex–neglects.*

There is, however, plenty of evidence that *t* was

not pronounced in the above words.   In the Alleyne
Papers the spelling *stricklier* is found (1608); in the
Verney Papers *respecks* (1629) and *respeck* (c. 1640
and 1647); *nex* (1647 and 1660, Verney Memoirs);
prospeck and *strick* in the early eighteenth-century
Wentworth Papers.   Many other spellings of a
similar kind have been noted at this period.   The
Grammarians also recognise this form of pronunciation.   Price says that *sex* and *sects*, *ax* and *acts*
sound alike; and Jones says that *-t* is omitted in
strict, direct, respect, sect, etc.

We may find it unpleasant to consider that our
great-grandfathers spoke in this way, but there is no
getting over a fact, in proof of which poets, letter-
writers, and Grammarians concur.

4. **Loss of -d after n finally, or before -s.**—Shakespeare rhymes *hounds–downs*; Swift, *Hammond–
backgammon.*   The loss of *-d* after *n* finally or before
-s is very old.   *Blyn,* ' blind,' occurs in the Norfolk
Guilds (1389); *pounse,* ' pounds,' in *Life of St.
Editha* (c. 1420); Margaret Paston writes *husbon*;
Machyn, *blyne,* ' blind '; the Alleyne Papers, *stannes,*
' stands,' and *hannes,* ' hands '; Lady Wentworth,
poun, ' pound.'   Cooper gives *thouzn* as the pronunciation of *thousand,* and Jones says *-d* is often
omitted in *beyond, Desmond, diamond,* etc.

5. **Loss of v before another consonant; of -th-
before -s.**—Spenser rhymes *trees–agreevs.*   He possibly pronounced the latter word ' *agrees.*'   The loss
of *r* is fairly common between vowels: Caxton has
pament, ' pavement '; Machyn, *Denshyre,* ' Devon-
shire '; Marston, *marle,* ' marvel '; Verney Memoirs,
senet, ' seven nights.'   None of these are exactly

parallel to the possible loss of *v* in *agreevs*.   A nearer
analogy is perhaps the loss of the *-th-* sound in the
plural *clothes*, which many still pronounce as ' *cloze*.'
Donne rhymes this word with *shows*; **Swift** with *beaus*;
Pope with *those*; **Goldsmith** with *goes*.   The sounds
v and *th* have in common that they are both voiced
open consonants, or, as some call them, ' spirants.'

Addition of a Consonant Finally after n.

Swift rhymes *ferment–vermin*, the latter word
being probably pronounced by him—*varmint*.   These
excrescent consonants *t* or *d* are very common after
n, l, etc., from the fifteenth century onwards.   The
very form *varment* occurs in a letter of Thomas
Pery (1539), and is put into the mouth of Tony
Lumpkin by **Goldsmith**.   There are many other
spellings of this kind: *orphant* in a letter of the Earl
of Shrewsbury (1582), and in Marston's ' Antonio
and Mellida ' (1602); Gabriel Harvey writes *surgiant*
for *surgeon*; and *sarment*, ' sermon,' is written by
Peter Wentworth (1711) and by Lady Wentworth
(1713); *gown'd,* ' gown,' is so spelt by one of the
Verney ladies in 1688, and by Lady Strafford in
1712.   **Swift** has *orphants* (' Ode to Sir W. Temple ');
Elphinstone (1783) considers *gownd* and *sermont*
as vulgarisms; and in 1814 Pegge says that *verment*
and *serment* are vulgar Londonisms.

Note on Swift's Pronunciation.

Swift's rhyme *slaughter–author* may well be an
Irishism, with *th* in the former word; on the other
hand, it may be based on an archaic pronunciation
of the second.

CHAPTER V

SPECIAL SEPARATE WORDS

Come (Infinitive and Present and Past Participle) and Some.

THE vowel sound in the present standard pronunciation of this word may be explained in either of two ways. It may be the normal descendant of that in O.E. *cuman, cume, -cumen* which, in M.E., sometimes remained unchanged, though often written *cŏme(n)*. On the other hand, M.E. *ŭ* in open syllables was, in many dialects, lengthened to *ō* and was levelled under the sound of M.E. *ō¹* (see pp. 75–81). This, as explained above (p. 76 [1]), became '*ū*'—- that is, the sound heard at present in *moon*, etc., in late M.E. This vowel, as shown on p. 76 [2] above, if shortened in the fifteenth century, acquires the sound of the vowel in *cut*, etc. Therefore the present sound in *come* may be derived from late M.E. *coome* with this early shortening. There is no doubt that a long type of the word, which can only be explained as from M.E. *coome*, was in use apparently down to Swift's time, in polite English, and may still be heard in the dialects. This form would stand in the same historical relation to our *come* as does *mood* to *flood* (see pp. 76, 77, etc., on this group of words). The vowel in *some* (O.E. *sŭm(e)*, M.E. *sōme*) may be explained in exactly the same way, and the long type, to judge by some of the rhymes, also survived. Unfortunately, collateral evidence from the Grammarians is lacking so far as I can see, but I am inclined to think that the following rhymes are based upon the long type just described.

Sackville, *come–doom–some*; Habington, *overcome–roome*; Waller, *come–room*; Cowley, *ibid.*; Swift *come–Rome* (see p. 128), *–gloom*; Pope, *come–doom*.

Devil.

1. O.E. *deofol* becomes M.E. *dēvel*, with *ē¹*, whence we should get, in Modern English, '*deevil.*'

2. But in the inflected forms—O.E. *deoflas*, plural, etc.—we get, in M.E., *devles*, with shortening of the vowel before *-fl-*. From this type our present standard form is derived.

3. Type 1, in the pronunciation of many speakers in the sixteenth century, underwent vowel shortening of the '*ee*' sound which resulted in a form which we may write '*divvle*' or '*divvil.*'

Types 2 and 3 survive in the dialects to-day.

In the sixteenth century Sir Thomas Smith writes *diuils* in his political tract, and Thomas Lever *diuilysh* in his sermons, which probably represent Type 3, though Smith, in his Grammar, indicates Type 1. In the next century the Grammarian Butler writes *deevil*, which he says ' comes from *eevil*, not *divel* as some far fetching it from *diabolus.*' Thus he knows Type 3, but prefers Type 1. Wharton also writes *deevil*.

Types 1 and 3 are both represented in the following rhymes:

Roister Doister, Shakespeare, and Byron all rhyme the word with *evil* (Type 1); Dryden and Pope with *civil* (Type 3).

Farthing.

Lord Rochester rhymes this word with *bear-garden*; **Pope** rhymes *farthing* with *garden*; **Swift** with *garden* and *Harding*. The pronunciation '*fardin*' is well established; **Machyn** writes *fardyng* (he, however, often writes *-yn* for *-ing—e.g., ridyn,* etc.); **Lady Wentworth** writes *fardin*.

Get.

Cowley rhymes *get* with *it*; **Dryden** with *writ*.

Mauger (1679) transcribes the English pronunciation of *get* for Frenchmen as *guit*; **Cooper** says that the word is pronounced *git*, ' facilitatis causa.'

Give, Live.

By the side of early modern *give*, which is the ancestor of our present type, there is evidence of the existence of another type of this word with the '*ee*' sound. This is the result of a process whereby early M.E. *ĭ* in open syllables was lengthened to *ē¹*, (for explanation of this symbol see p. 48, etc.), it came from M.E. *gĭve* whence *gēve*, whence the early modern form above. The same process has given us *week*—O.E. *wĭcu*, Early M.E. *wĭke*, Late *wēke*.

In the same way, by the side of *live* there was also a M.E. type *lēve*, which produced an early Modern form with the '*ee*' sound.

These forms, now unheard of in Standard English, are frequently found in the fifteenth, sixteenth, seventeenth, and eighteenth centuries in documents of all kinds, spelt *geue, geve, leue, leve*. The *geue* spellings may sometimes represent a form of quite different origin from that just described, but it is safe to assume that they often do represent the type under discussion. The Grammarians (Bullokar, 1580, and Gill, 1621) mention a pronunciation of *give* with the '*ee*' sound. *Leue,* etc., is found in Gregory, Margaret Paston, a Suffolk will of 1509, Machyn's Diary, the Verney Memoirs, and the Wentworth Papers. *Geue, forgeue,* etc., occur in Bury Wills (1509), etc., a letter of Sir Thomas More, Thomas Lever's sermons (1550), Latimer's sermons, Edward VI.'s First and Second Prayer Books, Ascham's *Scholemaster* and *Toxophilus,* Queen Elizabeth's letters, the Verney Memoirs, Mrs. Basire's letters, and the Wentworth Papers. In view of this evidence we shall consider the following rhymes normal. It will be noticed that even the poets sometimes write *geue, leue* according to the common habit of their age.

Rede me and be not wroth, *geue–greve, geue–to leue;* **Wyatt,** *geue–liue;* **Roister Doister,** *geue–greue, forgeue–leaue* (example of new pronunciation of *leave;* *cf.* pp. 61, 62); **Spenser,** *give–achieve;* **Habington,** *give–believe;* **Suckling,** *believe–live;* **Waller,** *retrieved–lived, give–believe, sleeve–give–leave;* **Cowley,** *give–leave, –eve, gives–deceives;* **Swift,** *believe him–forgive him.*

Gone.

This word is from O.E. *gān,* M.E. *gōn,* but the present forms require a word of explanation. There are two pronunciations current to-day among Standard English speakers—one which we may express roughly as ' gŏn,' the other which we may express as ' gawn.' The former is the result of a shortening

in the M.E. period, after which no further change
has occurred. The latter is due to a comparatively
recent lengthening of the vowel in this type. Compare the existing variants of *froth* and *frost*, where
the 'frawth,' 'frawst' types are also the result of a
late lengthening of M.E. *ŏ* (see pp. 96, 97).

In the sixteenth and seventeenth centuries a more
current type of *gone* was one which rhymed with
stone, a perfectly normal form. Just as O.E.
stān, M.E. *stōn* has resulted in *stone*, so we should
expect a modern *gone* with an identical vowel sound.
The following rhymes may be taken to represent
this type:

Roister Doister, *none–gone*; **Sackville,** *forgone–
bemoan, –alone, –one*; **Shakespeare,** *–one, –bone,
–alone*, also *–sun* (a faulty rhyme); **Drayton,** *–alone*;
Suckling, *–bemoan*; **Donne,** *–one*; **Milton,** *–grown*;
Waller, *–own*.

Half, Halves.

Dryden rhymes *halves–knaves*; **Swift,** *half–safe,
slaves–halves*.

We might be inclined to dismiss these as wholly
licentious rhymes were it not for the statement of
Coote (1627) that *hafe* for *half* is heard ' in the barbarous speech of your country people.' We may
further consider that we have to this day precisely
the same type as far as the vowel is concerned in the
word *ha'penny*. The loss of *f* in this is due to assimilation before *-p-*.

The vowel must go back to M.E. *ā*. The origin
of '*hafe*' must be M.E. *hălf*, whence, with loss of *l*,
and vowel lengthening *hāf*. Our pronunciation of
half, on the other hand, goes back to a M.E. type

without lengthening *hăf*. Historically, the type
' *hafe* ' is not only possible but still exists in the
truncated form mentioned. The reader must judge
whether the various considerations submitted above
are sufficient to establish that the rhymes of Dryden
and Swift are genuine. If the form required to
make them so existed as a current one in their days,
it is difficult to see why they should not have used it,
rather than insist on a pronunciation which, though
no doubt more usual, made no rhyme at all.

Heard.

The pronunciation of this word as *hard* is proved
by spellings and by the Grammarians' statements.
Such a pronunciation may be heard to-day among
educated people in Scotland. It is an example of
the M.E. change of -*ĕr*- to -*ar*-, discussed on pp. 83, 84.
The M.E. form is *herde*, and the spellings *harde, hard*
are very common in private documents, and even in
published works from the fifteenth to the eighteenth
century. It is used by persons of every class—
Margaret Paston, the Celys, Lord Berners, Sir Thomas
Elyot, Cranmer, Machyn, Latimer, Gabriel Harvey,
Lord Burghley, the Verneys, and Lady Wentworth,
to mention no more. There cannot be the slightest
doubt that it was the current colloquial form in
good and educated society. *Hard* is further recognised by Grammarians such as Gill, who calls it
' corrupt,' by Butler, Hodges, Price, Cooke, Cooper,
and Jones. The rhymes with the ' hard ' type must
be fairly common, though I have only noted the
following :

Spenser rhymes *heard* with *regard*; **Shakespeare**

with *ward* (see p. 67, etc.) and *regard*; **Dryden** with *reward* (see p. 70) and *guard*. Dryden's rhyme *preferred–heard* is almost certainly of the same type (see p. 84). Spenser also rhymes *heard* with *reard*, which points to a different type, probably the ancestor of our present form.

Dr. Johnson is said to have pronounced the word ' *heer'd* ' as being closer to the spelling than *hard*. The same pronunciation is evidently the basis of Pope's rhyme *heard–revered*.

Height, High.

The early M.E. forms of these words are *hēhthe*, etc., and *hēh*, *hēz* respectively. In some dialects M.E. *ē* before *h* or *z* becomes *ī*, in others it remains or is diphthongised to *ēi*. The word *eye* is from M.E. *ēze*, whence later *ize* on the one hand and *ēye* on the other. Chaucer's scribes often write *eye*, but his rhymes show that the poet pronounced the *ī* type which, of course, is the ancestor of the modern pronunciation of *eye*, though, as often in the Chaucer MSS., the other type is recorded in the spelling. Our pronunciation of *high* is from the old *ī* type, as is that of *height*, though in the latter word the spelling preserves a different type. Had the M.E. *heiz*, *heizthe* type been preserved, they would now be pronounced like ' *hay*,' ' *hate*.' That these types actually did survive alongside of the other down to the early eighteenth century is shown both by rhymes and by the Grammarians' statements.

Price puts *high* and *hay* together as having the same sound; Cooper equates the vowel sound in *weight, height,* and *convey*; Baker says that *height* is pronounced both ' *hait* ' and ' *hite.* '

Drayton rhymes *height* with *streight*; **Waller** with *strait*; **Dryden** with *fate.*

Oblige.

Pope has at least two examples of this word rhyming with *besiege,* one of which—that in the ' Epistle to Dr. Arbuthnut,' ll. 207-208:

> Fearing e'vn fools, by flatterers besieged
> And so obliging that he ne'er obliged—

is well known; the other is *besiege ye–oblige ye* (' Imitations of Horace,' book i., epistle vii., 29-30).

It has been said that the pronunciation ' *obleege* ' was killed, as a fashionable form, by the ridicule of Lord Chesterfield. The only objections to this view are first that the pronunciation did *not* die out in good society for nearly a hundred years after Lord Chesterfield's letter in which he refers to the word; and secondly, that although there must be a certain ambiguity in his lordship's expression, since some have read it as a condemnation, others, including the present writer, have no doubt that the type of pronunciation condemned is not ' *obleeged,*' but the alternative pronunciation which everyone now uses.

What Lord Chesterfield (in 1749) says is this— he is speaking of the ' vulgar man '—' even his pronunciation of proper words carries the mark of the beast along with it. He calls the earth *yearth*, he is *obleiged,* not obliged to you.' It will be noted that it is in expressing the ' vulgar ' pronunciation *yearth* that the writer departs from the orthodox spelling, not in that of the ' correct ' form. It is reasonable to suppose that he does the same for the other word, and that *obleige* is intended to express the reprehensible type. There is an interesting entry in Coleridge's ' Table Talk' under the date December 29, 1822, which appears to confirm the view here taken that *obleege* long continued to be the fashionable type:

' Dear Charles Mathews told me he was once performing privately before the King. The King was much pleased with the imitation of Kemble and said: " I liked Kemble very much. He was one of my earliest friends. I remember he was once talking, and found himself out of snuff. I offered him my box. He declined taking any; ' He, a poor actor, could not put his fingers into a royal box.' I said: ' Take some pray; you will *obleege* me.' " Upon which Kemble replied: " It would become your royal mouth better to say, *oblige* me," and took a pinch.' The King referred to must be George IV.—he was probably still Prince of Wales at the time of the incident he narrates, though King at the time of Mathews' private performance. Allowing for the probability of royal personages in that age being inclined to archaic pronunciation, it is hardly conceivable that George IV. should still have retained a pronunciation which Lord Chesterfield had made unfashionable after the middle eighteenth century. Kemble is more likely to have been a purist in pronunciation than the King, and by his time ' *obleeged* ' was probably becoming old-fashioned, and very possibly survived, as is often the case with speech forms, only among the highest classes of all, and in the lowest. There are half a dozen examples of such spellings as *obleg, obledged, disablegin,* and so on, in the Verney Memoirs between 1647-1666. There are also some writers in these papers, including Sir Ralph Verney, who spell *obleiged,* which may represent a pronunciation similar to our own.

One, None.

The normal form of this word in the London dialect would be that which survives in *on-ly* and *al-one*— that is to say, we should have expected it to be pronounced so as to rhyme with *stone,* and so on. The present-day pronunciation has got into Standard English from some Regional Dialect, probably from the South-West. The ancestor of this form is found about 1420 in *Life of St. Editha* (Wilts), several times written *won.* Spellings with *w-* occur in letters of Henry VIII., in Queen Elizabeth's translations, in Latimer's sermons, in Machyn's diary, in Verney Memoirs, and the Wentworth Papers.

But while our present form was gaining ground the old pronunciation long survived. Among seventeenth-century Grammarians Hodges gives *owne* and *one* as 'near alike,' Price as identical in sound; Wallis says that *one* and *none* have '*ô* rotundum,' other examples of which are *pole, boat, oat, chose;* Cooper pairs *one* and *own* as being pronounced alike. The Writing Scholar's Companion (1695) actually regards '*wun,*' which is meant to represent the present type, as vulgar. Rather an out-of-date view, seeing it was the form of Henry VIII and Elizabeth.

The vowel sound in *none* must be due to the

analogy of *one*. This word also retains its old form in the seventeenth century, as we see from Wallis. In the following the old pronunciation of both words is evidently used by the poets:

Roister Doister, *alone–one, none–gone* (see p. 120). **Wyatt,** *none–mone*. **Sackville,** *one–stone, mone; none–mone; forgone–alone*. **Shakespeare,** *one–gone, bone; none–gone*. **Cowley,** *grown–one*; **Dryden,** *thrown–one*. **Pope's** *one–undone* evidently exhibits our present type of the former word. **Milton's** *one–soon* may represent a *w* type of the first word, and a short vowel (*ŭ*) like ours in *pull* in both words. The absence of unrounding may be explained by the influence of the initial '*w*' sound. The form of *soon* here suggested would show the later shortening (*cf.* pp. 76, 77).

Passed, Past.

Shakespeare rhymes *past* with *waste* (in the sonnet 'When in the Chronicle of Wasted Time'), and **Dryden** *passed* with *embraced*. Hodges says that *past* and *paste* are pronounced 'near alike.' This would make the rhymes good if true, but can it be justified historically? I venture to suggest that there was a confusion between the two M.E. words *pācen*, whence our *pace*, and *păssen*, whence our *pass*. These two words, which have a common origin, are both used by Chaucer in the sense of *pass, pass out, away*, etc. If Shakespeare and Dryden, in the above rhymes, are using the forms of *pace* with the sense of *pass*, although the latter be written, and if this practice is at the basis of Hodges' statement, then the matter is clear, and the rhymes are true ones.

Phlegm.

Swift rhymes this word with *supreme*, and **Pope** with *extreme*. Baker, in 1724, says it is pronounced *fleem*, and several earlier Grammarians make similar statements.

Pour.

The origin of this word is very doubtful. **Drayton** rhymes it with *Stour* (the river), and **Cowley** with *shower*.

The Grammarians Hodges, Price, and Cooper all say the pronunciation is identical with that of *power*. I used to hear this pronunciation as a boy from a very vulgar speaker.

Rome.

Our present pronunciation of this word is not the traditional English form, but borrowed from the French. The O.E. and M.E. forms had $\bar{o}^1$, which normally developed into the vowel sound in *doom*, etc. (*cf*. pp. 76, etc.). Hodges, Cooper, and Jones all agree that in their days the word was pronounced with ' *oo* ' long. This old, traditional pronunciation is reflected in the rhymes.

Shakespeare rhymes it with *doom, groom*; **Donne** with *roome* and *come* (see pp. 117, 118); **Cowley** and **Dryden** have apparently the new-fangled pronunciation, and rhyme it with *home*; **Swift** with *gloom* and *doom*; **Pope** with *doom*.

Realm.

The present pronunciation of this word is so well fixed that we are apt to forget that the introduction of *l* is comparatively recent.

In the fourteenth century Langland, Wyclif, and Chaucer have such forms as *reame, reume, rēme*. Note the latter's rhyme (' None Preestes Tale,' ll. 315-316) :

> *Wher they ne felte noon effect in drēmes*
> *Who-so wol sēken actes of sondry rēmes.*

In 1627, Coote, always a stickler for a distinguished form of speech, gives *ream* for *realm* as an example of ' the barbarous speech of your country people.'

Hodges, less exacting, simply states that *ream* and *realm* are identical.

Rede me and be not wroth rhymes *realm* with *beame*; **Sackville** with *streame* and *eame* (uncle); and **Drayton** with *stream*.

Should, Would, Could.

The sound of *l* is not normally lost before *-d* in stressed syllables. The present *l*-less forms of the two first words are probably to be explained as arising in unstressed positions. As these words occur rather more commonly in ordinary speech without stress than with it, the old stressed forms have been lost and the unstressed forms have become the sole forms in use.

The spellings without *l* appear in Elyot's *Gouernour* (1531), in Gabriel Harvey's letters (1573-1580) (*shudd*), and in Verney Memoirs (1642) (*shud*); *wode* and *wood* occur in the Verney Memoirs (1656).

As against this the early poets frequently rhyme *should* and *would* with words which, so far as we know, always have been pronounced with *l*.

Wyatt, *would–hold–behold* (' Tottel,' p. 57); *should–behold* (p. 68); *–gold* (p. 87). **Spenser,** *should–hold–*

gold (' Ruins of Time '). **Shakespeare,** *should–cool'd* (' Venus and Adonis,' l. 385, etc.). **Drayton,** *would–hold* (' Polyolbion,' Book 22). **Waller,** however, has *would–mud* (' Summer Island,' ll. 49-50).

Could.

This word, from M.E. *coud(e)*, owes its *l* entirely to the analogy of *should* and *would*, and many have supposed that this was purely graphic, but the following rhymes awake our curiosity:

Spenser, *could–behold* (' Hours of Bewtie'); **Drayton,** *could–behold* (' Polyolbion,' Book 17); **Dryden,** rhymes *could–good*.

The evidence of the Grammarians is not very full, but it seems to establish that forms with and without *l* existed in seventeenth-century pronunciations. Hodges says that *would* is pronounced like *wood* and *wooed*; Price, on the other hand, puts *could*, *cold*, and *cool'd* together; Wharton writes *woold*, *coold*, *shoold* as representing the pronunciation; while Cooper says that *could* sounds like *cool'd*.

It appears, then, that unless the poets were guilty of pure eye-rhymes in the instances cited, and unless the Grammarians are deceiving themselves and us, not only was *l* sounded by some speakers as late as the last quarter of the seventeenth century, but this pronunciation was even extended to *could*.

It should be noted that the *l* pronunciation of *should* and *would* is natural in rhymes so long as the distinction between the stressed and unstressed pronunciations persisted, since rhyming words are stressed; and, further, that *l* might survive longer in rhymes than elsewhere, partly on this account and partly owing to poetical tradition.

Show.

This word, formerly also spelt *shew*, had, in M.E. and Early Modern English, two pronunciations: (1) the ancestor of our own, and another (2) which, in the sixteenth and seventeenth centuries, was identical with *shoe*. These are derived from two different (late O.E.?) types—*scéāwian*, which gave M.E. *schēwen*, whence *shew=shoe* (as Price, 1668, describes it), and *scéāwean*, with shifting of stress to the second element of the diphthong, whence M.E. *shōwen* and modern *show*, as at present. The *shew* spelling survived long after the other, our present pronunciation, was the only one in use. In the sixteenth and seventeenth centuries the word rhymes both with *dew*, etc., and with *woe*, etc., the former being perhaps more frequent. Type (2) is recognised by the Grammarians Salesbury, Bullokar, Gill, Price, Cooper, and Jones. The spelling *shew*, a traditional one, is itself practically phonetic, but *shued* in the Verney Memoirs (1663) is unmistakable.

Both types appear in the following rhymes (the rhyming words alone are given):

Rede me and be not wroth, *Mathewe*; **Spenser,** *vew*, 'view,' *bestowe*, *belowe*; **Drayton,** *grew*; **Donne,** *flow*; **Milton,** *shewth–youth–ruth*, *shew– renew*, *dew*; **Waller,** *grow*; **Cowley,** *do*, *shews– woes*, *shew him–to him*, *brow* (a bad rhyme unless the rhyming word be pronounced according to Northern type); **Swift,** *shewing–wooing*.

Wont (' accustomed ').

The old pronunciation, still heard not very l ong
ago from very old people, survives in **Spenser's**
and **Milton's** rhyme of this word with *hunt*.   Milton's
contemporary, Wharton, includes it in a list containing *month, honie, monie*, which, according to
him, all have the same sound.   This is perfectly
normal.   *Wont* is historically a Present Participle
formation from O.E. (*ge*)*wunian*, 'to be in the habit
of, accustom oneself to ' (*cf.* O.E. *wuna*, M.E. *wŏne*,
' habit, custom ').   Our modern pronunciation, which
rhymes with *don't*, is not traditional, but is based on
the spelling.

Would (see under 'Should' above).

Wound (' vulnus '), etc.

It is supposed that the present-day pronunciation of this word is due to the influence of *w-*, whereby
the vowel in M.E. *wūnd*(*e*) underwent no diphthong-
ing in some dialects, but remained unaltered.   On
the other hand, among many speakers in the sixteenth and seventeenth centuries the word was
pronounced with the same diphthong as in *bound*,
etc., like other words which had *ū* in M.E.

All the poets rhyme this word with *sound, found,
ground*, etc., and very rarely with such words as
swoonde.   I have, however, noted *wounds–lampoons*
in **Lord Rochester's** *Rehearsal*.   The old pronunciation still survives in dialects, in the obsolescent
'*zounds*, and I heard it a year ago, in *wound* itself,
from a very accomplished American lady.

Yellow.

Swift, in lines ' To Betty,' rhymes this word with *tallow*. Jones gives the pronunciation as *yallow*, which would make a perfect rhyme. As a matter of fact, Swift probably said ' *yaller–taller*.' Howel (1662) says that *tallow* and *hollow* end in short *u*, which doubtless means the common English 'murmur vowel.' The syllable *-ow*, when unstressed, was early pronounced with this reduced vowel, as appears from Bokenam's *felas*, ' fellows ' (1443), and much later from Pope's rhyme *fellow–prunella*, and from Swift's *tell us–fellows*.

Yes.

Swift rhymes this word with *dismiss*. ' *Yis* ' is said by Sheridan (in 1780), and ' *is* ' by Jones (in 1701) to be the sound of the word.

Yet.

Cowley rhymes this word with *it*, and Dryden with *writ* and *unfit*. The pronunciation intended is undoubtedly ' *yit*,' a dialectal variant frequently used by Chaucer, recognised by Smith in the sixteenth century, and in 1621 by Gill. The form *it* is recorded by Hodges and Price later in the seventeenth century.

INDEX OF RHYMES

above–*move*, 81
abroad–*understood*, 82
adust–*worst*, 113
after–*dafter*, 111
aggrieves–*trees*, 115
aiding–*reading*, 54
air–*dear*, –*severe*, 66
ale–*veal*, 54
all–*shall*, 107
alone–*gone*, 121
already–*greedy*, 89
appear–*bear*, –*swear*, 66
appears–*forbears*, 66
archer–*searcher*, 84
are–*wear* (vb.), –*compare*, –*unaware*, –*snare*, –*fair*, –*declare*, 105; –*prayer*, –*care*, –*were*, –*fair*, –*pair*, –*aware*, –*spare*, –*despair*, –*here*, –*there*, –*bear*, 106
are–*war*, 69
art–*desert*, 84
assoil–*compile*, –*awhile*, –*toil*, 75
author–*slaughter*, 116
aware–*are*, 106

backgammon–*Hammond*, 115
barrel–*quarrel*, 69
be–*sea*, 60
beads–*maids*, 53
beam–*realm*, 129
beams–*Thames*, 53
bear–*are*, 106; –*dear*, –*here*, 60; –*hear*, 65
bears–*spears*, 65, 66; –*peers*, –*ears*, 66
beasts–*guests*, 98
beat–*fleet* (n.), 60
beat (pret. and p.p.)–*set*, 92

beaten–*threaten*, 89
beaver–*favour*, 54
beech–*wych*, 94
beheld–*seeld*, 102
bemoan–*swollen*, 114
beneath–*death*, –*breath*, –*bequeath*, 89
beseech–*reach*, 60
beseech thee–*teach thee*, 60
bleeds–*sheds*, 60
blood–*good*, –*stood*, –*wood*, 81; –*crowd*, 82
boast–*tossed*, –*lost*, 98
brave–*have*, 106
bread–*feed*, 60, 89
break–*betake*, 53; –*undertake*, 54
breath–*wreath*, –*bequeath*, –*beneath*, –*heath*, –*death*, 89
brood–*flood*, 81
bud–*good*, 81
buds–*woods*, 81
build–*field*, 103
builds–*shields*, –*yields*, –*fields*, 103
burst–*dust*, 114

Cæsar–*phrase are*, 54
care–*fear*, 66; –*are*, 106
career–*there*, 66
cares–*tears*, 66
carve–*serve*, 84
cease–*plaice*, –*peace*, 54
cease–*these*, 60
ceas'd–*rais'd*, 53; –*rest*, –*best*, 92
ceased–*placed*, 54
charge ye–*clergy*, 84
cheap–*rape*, 54
cheat–*great*, 52